ON CREATIVITY

ALSO IN THE SERIES

ON CREATIVITY

Edited by

SUDHIR KAKAR &
GÜNTER BLAMBERGER

PENGUIN

VIKING

An imprint of Penguin Random House

VIKING

USA | Canada | UK | Ireland | Australia
New Zealand | India | South Africa | China | Singapore

Viking is part of the Penguin Random House group of companies
whose addresses can be found at global.penguinrandomhouse.com

Published by Penguin Random House India Pvt. Ltd
4th Floor, Capital Tower 1, MG Road,
Gurugram 122 002, Haryana, India

Penguin
Random House
India

First published in Viking by Penguin Books India 2015
Introduction copyright © Sudhir Kakar and Günter Blamberger 2015
The copyright for individual pieces vests with the individual authors or their estates.

SPONSORED BY THE

Federal Ministry
of Education
and Research

INTERNATIONALES KOLLEG MORPHOMATA

The views and opinions expressed in this book are the authors' own and the facts are as
reported by them which have been verifed to the extent possible, and the publishers are
not in any way liable for the same.

ISBN 9780670088072

Typeset in Joanna MT by Manipal Digital Systems
Printed at Replika Press Pvt. Ltd, India

www.penguin.co.in

MIX
Paper from
responsible sources
FSC® C016779

This is a legitimate digitally printed version of the book and therefore might not
have certain extra finishing on the cover.

Contents

Introduction

Sudhir Kakar and Günter Blamberger

The concept of genius has undoubtedly been one of the most influential concepts in the European theory of the arts, dating in various forms from the eighteenth century. It is also intrinsically linked to the philosophy of the subject. In the twentieth century, psychological studies on creativity, which took the artistic genius as a role model for their inquiries into the personal origin of fundamental innovations in all domains, were still centred on the notion of an individual creator in science, art and technology. The Western theory of creativity as personal ingenuity was globally influential although it is obvious that it does not fit into traditional Eastern understanding and practices of creativity. Moreover, in the meantime, this model of creativity also fails to account for some of the current Western practices of creativity as a collaborative effort, or network creativity, in many fields of innovation.

An international conference was therefore held in Wasan Island, Canada, in July 2012, to find contemporary answers to the question of how newness enters the world. This volume, reflecting the proceedings of the conference, is in two parts. The essays of Sudhir Kakar, Günter Blamberger and Weihua Niu have a cross-cultural perspective. They compare historical and actual concepts of creativity in the East and the West. The essays of Patrick Mahony, Margaret Boden and James Kaufman are from an interdisciplinary perspective. They demonstrate the successes and limits of the psychoanalytical and psychological approaches as master discourses of creativity studies in the twentieth century, and discuss the approach of cognitive biology as seemingly the most promising avenue for solving the mystery of the creative mind in the twenty-first century.

Creativity research in a cross-cultural perspective

Sudhir Kakar's essay compares Western theories of creativity with those of Hindu tradition. The focus of Western theories has been the creative person. Psychoanalysis has continued this tradition by emphasizing the biographical roots of creativity, tracing its source to the creative person's emotional conflicts and highlighting the therapeutic function of creativity. There has recently been a shift from the psychological to the biological in that the special nature of the creative person's cognitive and perceptual processes is receiving greater attention. On the other hand, Indian foundational texts on creativity do not concentrate on the personality of the creative person which needs to be transcended for creativity to flower. Creativity arises from his or her participation in a transcendent-spiritual unconscious. Kakar then looks at an anthropological study of traditional painters and the views of Rabindranath Tagore—perhaps the greatest creative genius produced by India in the last two hundred years—to discuss the contemporary relevance of the traditional Indian view of creativity.

Günter Blamberger analyses the mythological, social and philosophical backgrounds of the Western idea of the autonomous genius who is allegedly capable of producing 'original' compositions according to the Biblical myth of the divine 'creation out of nothing'. In critical revisions of historical testimonies (Cézanne, Dürer, Kant, Sorescu, Brecht, Kleist, Shaffer, Guilford, etc.), Blamberger demonstrates the ultimate hopelessness of investigating the personal origin of creativity which is still the focus of psychological studies of creativity. He pleads for a paradigm shift by moving the analytical focus from the personal origin of creativity to the process of creativity. He argues that creativity is not an independent cognitive competence preceding all action, simply 'translating' itself into practical activities or media. Creativity is experience, it is a knowledge to be generated out of practice, a knowledge that is dependent on the medium and the material of its expression, on social interaction and mainly on the occupational domain in which one becomes creative. Blamberger shows this by using, as example, film production as a process of shared agencies. In most workplaces today, a theory of creativity can no longer refer to an individual because the creative processes are based on a division of labour within collective and dynamic networks. But it is also obvious that cooperative processes of creation in film presumably function differently from those in industrial laboratories, management or sports. 'Workplace studies' and 'theories of practice' are necessary for discovering the different logics of creativity. Thus, creativity is both a trans-disciplinary and a cross-cultural problem. It is a paradox that the Confucian and the Taoist understandings of creativity as co- or contextual creativity seem to be more appropriate to current Western practices of creativity than the traditional Western approaches.

Weihua Niu's essay proposes that there is a unique concept called 'Chinese creativity' which is different from the Western notion of creativity. Chinese creativity stresses that creative products have a stronger impact on society than the individual who creates the product. Chinese society also historically places moral standards as important characteristics of creative individuals, and believes that ethical conduct is an inseparable part of one's creativity. There are also some variations among different sub-societies in contemporary Chinese societies, including Mainland China, Taiwan, Hong Kong, and other parts of the world. Weihua Niu believes that these features are associated with the philosophical roots of the Chinese notion of creativity and the interaction between the Western and the Eastern worlds.

Creativity in an interdisciplinary perspective

Patrick Mahony, psychoanalyst and literary scholar, draws up a balanced account of Sigmund Freud's creativity. His essay is in three parts: a positive roll call of Freud's known and lesser-known attributes and achievements which have contributed to the betterment of society; then, a disarming catalogue of his negative attitudes which would appear to undermine the possibility of any cultural contribution; and lastly, a focus on two sexually oriented mindsets which both informed Freud's creative dilemmas and facilitated his creativity.

Margaret Boden, a prominent expert in computer models of the mind, advances the argument that creativity is likely to remain a neuroscientific mystery for many years to come since, of the three types of creativity—combinational, exploratory and transformational—only the first has been significantly illuminated by neuroscience. And even the combinational is not fully understood in neural terms. The other two are even more recalcitrant. This is due to difficulty in defining thinking styles in arts or science, and in identifying the various computational processes which are involved in using them. Without doing that, helpful neuroscientific questions simply cannot arise. One key problem to which Boden points is that hierarchical systems—including many creative 'styles'—cannot yet be effectively represented by (connectionist) computer models inspired by the neural networks in the brain. Another is the difficulty of explaining the recognition of relevance in computational/theoretical terms.

James Kaufman, one of the leading American psychologists of creativity, first summarizes his Amusement Park Theoretical (APT) model of creativity, which integrates the generalist and domain-specific approaches to creativity. He then presents his Four C model of creativity which fills in the gaps between Big-C or the creativity of a genius and little-c or everyday creativity with two additional categories: mini-c—the novel and personally meaningful self-discoveries—and Pro-c or professional level creativity of those who have not yet achieved the level of Big-C creators of genius.

All the contributions in this volume were first given as talks at the international conference, On Creativity, in Wasan Island. The concept of the conference was drawn up by Sudhir Kakar and Günter Blamberger at the Centre for Advanced Studies in the Humanities at the University of Cologne, Germany (Internationales Kolleg Morphomata). Preference was given to a location in North America, where creativity research is much more prevalent than in Europe.

We are deeply indebted to Breuninger Stiftung for providing the generous support which made holding the conference possible; our personal thanks go especially to Helga Breuninger and Volker Hann. Furthermore, we owe a debt of gratitude to the Federal Ministry of Education and Research (BMBF), Germany, which has been funding the Cologne Centre for Advanced Studies since its inception in 2009. The name 'Morphomata' is the ancient Greek word for forming aesthetic ideas in works of art and literature; for thinking images; for figurations of lasting cultural impact, like the figurations of creativity which we are analysing in this book, which, too, is financed by the BMBF. Finally, we wish to express our thanks to all the contributors to this volume and to Ambar Sahil Chatterjee, Editor, Penguin Books India.

The Artistic Genius: Western and Indian Perspectives

Sudhir Kakar

My interest in the artistic genius is not in his or her creative *potential* which is marked by a gift for reinterpreting what is taken for granted, a propensity to search for and resolve contradictions, an aptitude for coining metaphors and connecting unrelated ideas in a novel way. Nor am I interested in the creative *mindset* which is said to be domain-specific and has such features as 'wonderment, independence, nonconformity, flexibility . . . capability for relaxation',[1] to which I would also add playfulness. My focus here is on the extraordinary creative *person*, the creative genius whose exceptional contributions— sometimes even across domains—are acknowledged as revolutionary and which have lastingly altered the landscape of his or her domain. I wish to address in this essay what I would call the cultural psychology of the artist and artistic creativity by taking examples from European and Hindu Indian traditions.

For a long time, Western notions of the genius—influenced by Plato and Aristotle—linked one's extraordinary creativity to an extreme mental state.[2] The madness in Plato's poetry was attributed to the gods taking over his personality and speaking through him, while the melancholy of the genius, from Aristotle onwards (including Plato and Socrates among the melancholics), was attributed to an excess of bodily humour, black bile.[3] Indeed, in the European Middle Ages and early modern period, melancholy—exemplified in Albrecht Dürer's well-known portrait of a man sunk in melancholic thought as the quintessential representation of the artist—became the defining attribute of the creative person.

Beginning with Freud's 1910 study of Leonardo da Vinci, the admixture of mania and depression as a defining attribute of a genius was expanded by psychoanalysts. Rather than viewing it as a fixed psychopathological structure in the creative writer's or artist's psyche, they now focused their attention on major emotional conflicts as the source of his or her creativity. These conflicts, which have their source in the artist's childhood and early youth, are expressed by the creative person in his or her work, poetry, music or art, while, at the same time, creativity and the creative product buffer him or her from the trauma inherent in the emotional conflict. This function of creativity, which acts as a haven from the storms of emotional life and the swirling of subterranean passions, is not limited to artists but may well extend to all highly creative individuals. As Albert Einstein observes, 'Man seeks to form for himself, in whatever manner is suitable for him, a simplified and lucid image of the world [Bild der Welt], and so to overcome the world of experience by striving to replace it to some extent by this image. That is what the painter does, and the poet, the speculative philosopher, the natural scientist, each in his own way. Into this [simplified and lucid] image of the world and its formation, he places the center of gravity of his emotional life, in order to attain the peace and serenity that he cannot find within the narrow confines of swirling personal experience.'[4]

In the West, the therapeutic function of creativity has been highlighted by many. The German poet Heinrich Heine writes:

Disease may well have been the ground
In full for that creative urge,
Creation was my body's purge,
Creating I've grown sane and sound.

It is a sentiment echoed by the Austrian poet, Rainer Maria Rilke: 'My work is really nothing but a self-treatment', and by the novelist Graham Greene: 'Writing is a form of therapy; sometimes I wonder how all those who do not write, compose or paint can manage to escape madness, the melancholia, the panic fear which is inherent in the human situation'.[5] But, the self-healing process is not always successful and artists are sometimes prone to exaggerating the benefit of their creativity. Art, even in the presence of considerable talent, cannot always stabilize a disintegrating personality. Artistic creativity, as the Canadian psychoanalyst Patrick Mahony observes, though potentially effective in various degrees in regulating symptoms or even providing a narcissistically comforting insight, cannot produce a deep and permanent structural change in the psyche.[6] On the other hand, it is true that for certain artists, not to write, paint, sculpt or make music may lead to drastic psychic disintegration. Thus, although the American poet Sylvia Plath referred to 'poetry as therapy' and the English writer Virginia Woolf relied on her 'art to keep [her] head sane', both women committed suicide.[7] (Parenthetically, let me note that ancient textbooks of Sanskrit poetics, too, recognize what they call 'escape from ills' as one of the secondary reasons why a poet writes poetry.[8])

More recent psychoanalytic contributions to the creative personality have highlighted factors other than emotional conflict: the availability—beyond childhood—of 'transitional' space (Winnicott) where play and creativity have their home; 'self-effectance' or the faith in one's own genius, which is then an autonomous source of self-esteem; the functioning of the artwork as a 'self-object' (Kohut); enhancing the creative personality's psychic integration and sense of being alive; as also the 'mirroring' appreciation of the audience which performs the same function.[9] And though the special nature of his perception and cognition are currently receiving the greatest attention, for me, the compelling *story* of a genius remains a narration of his developmental experiences which were vital for the flowering of his creativity.

Contemporary contributions to the riddle of artistic creativity seek to complement the role of emotions (when they do not replace it altogether), which biography can bring out vividly, with the special nature of the artist's cognitive and perceptual processes which have their source in the brain; the shift is from the psyche of the creative personality to its soma. In other words, creativity is viewed by many as fundamentally biological. Indeed, together with the mystery of consciousness, the riddle of creativity is currently the Holy Grail of biology.

For instance, synesthesia, the blending of senses, is said to be seven to eight times higher in artists than in other people. Synesthesia increases the skill in forming metaphors, that is, the linking in the brain of seemingly unrelated concepts. The neuroscientist, V.S. Ramachandran, suggests that there may be a gene, which, if expressed in one part of the brain—the fusiform gyrus—results in a lower synesthesia. If expressed in another part—the angular gyrus—it results in a higher synesthesia. If expressed in the entire brain, we get the potential artist.[10] There is also evidence that artists can shift between brain hemispheres more fluidly than non-artists and that creativity may be enhanced when interhemispheric flexibility is maximized. And although there are influential voices, such as that of the philosopher McGinn, who argue that the explanation of high-level thought and consciousness is as far beyond the cognitive capacities of *Homo sapiens* as theoretical physics is beyond the capacities of squirrels and chimpanzees, there is a widespread belief that neurosciences hold the key to the understanding of extraordinary creativity.[11] Creativity is not mysterious and, as the Nobel Laureate Pete Medawar observes, the idea that 'creativity is beyond analysis is a romantic illusion we must now outgrow'.[12]

On the other hand, Indian foundational texts on high-level artistic creativity take a very different tack from that of the Western tradition. From the classical text on the performing arts, Bharata's *Natya Shastra* (ca. 200 BC), through its authoritative interpretation in the commentary by Abhinavagupta (975–1025 AD), who included literature and fine arts in his theory of aesthetics, to the modern works of the renowned art historian Ananda Coomaraswamy (1877–1947), there has been a unitary view of the creative artist. He is not a flawed being, prone to madness or melancholia. Not for the Indian artist the sensual excesses that Europeans have almost come to expect of their creative artists. The ancient texts, the *Shilpa Shastras*, describe the Indian artist thus: 'The painter must be a good man, no sluggard, nor given to anger; holy, learned, self-controlled, devout and charitable,' and especially not an adulterer.[13] In an artist, striving for individuality, receiving nutrients for self-esteem from 'effectance' and appreciation of the audience were suspicious. To be truly creative, it was necessary for individual personality traits and complexes to be transcended. As Coomaraswamy observes, 'The Indian artist, though a person, is not a personality.'[14] They were believed to be transitory and accidental, veiling the fount of creativity, *pratibha*, creative imagination, the faculty capable of creating novel combinations of ideas and images. Pratibha is an inborn faculty due to impressions of past births that are so strong in the artist that it responds to the slightest stimuli, which are normally ignored by others.

Is the traditional Indian view of the artist and artistic creativity still relevant for artists in contemporary India?

The only empirical study I know is an older one, from the 1970s, of 155 traditional painters, all men, from Nathdwara, a temple town and pilgrimage centre in the state of Rajasthan.[15] According to the best of these painters, recognized by their peers as 'masters', artistic creativity has five major sources:

- *An innate creative drive*, analogous to the pratibha of classical texts, into which one may tap through hard work and 'right living'. Many of them likened themselves to passive instruments through which this creative drive works. They mention being in touch with a different world, one full of primordial images, symbols and 'root emotions' (*jarh, rasik*). Others view it as an internal reservoir of creative power (*maya rupa*) which is a storehouse of imagination (*kalpana shakti*), which is also manifested in dreams, visions and delusions.

A painter explains the notion thus:

> Creativity? Oh! It's all maya rupa, everything. This maya which I have inside me is thrown into my art. This is a sacred truth. All imagination and things of worldly appearance and form first exist there. They are not real when they come outside. These appearances in art are confused thinking, fantasies, and like a dream world. All outside forms are determined by the same maya force.

They are all from maya—from inside. The whole world is, furthermore, nothing more than God's own maya creation. It is the dream of Brahman and we painters contain a part of that force in us because we are all part of Brahman (universal soul).[16]

Pratibha and maya rupa, then, constitute the mysterious artistic gift which Freud famously admitted (though he later changed his mind) were beyond the capacity of psychoanalysis to elucidate.[17]

- *Participation in a sacred mystery*. Through yogic discipline and inner searching, the artist reaches a stage where, as a subject, he merges with the inner object or emotional state which he would like to render into concrete form.
- *Psychological balance*, through a confrontation between and a union of opposites in the psyche of the artist. As one of the most creative artists put it, 'In order to have success, the creative artist must confront and unite the opposites in himself, no matter how antagonistic to each other they are.'[18] Another observes: 'My nature is balanced because it is neither passive and inert nor overly active and aggressive, it is between these two extremes.'[19] The process is believed to flower with age.

These opposites are mainly the male and female principles. Artists say that creative potential is actualized when the female power, shakti—represented by the goddess Saraswati, the goddess of knowledge, music and arts—is symbolically integrated with the male principle, which, in the case of artists is represented by the god Vishwakarma, presiding deity of architects and craftsmen, a form of the creator Brahma, her father and consort. From the moment a sperm fertilizes an ovum, something new—a third original something—emerges. It is the same with artistic creativity, the symbolic third springing from the union of opposites, called *dhvani* or *dhvanit*.

- *A special part of heredity*, artists claiming direct descent from Vishwakarma.
- *The realm of Kama or Eros.*

Here, the close relationship between artistic creativity and the sexual life of the artist is often mentioned. Not in the sense of sublimation, but of the libido released through sexual activity which spills into and fuels artistic creativity. In this case, Indian painters seem to endorse Freud's observation: 'The relationship between the amount of sublimation possible and the amount of sexual activity necessary naturally varies very much from person to person and even from one calling to another. An abstinent artist is hardly conceivable; but an abstinent young savant is certainly no rarity. The latter can, by his self-restraint, liberate forces for his studies; while the former probably finds his artistic achievements powerfully stimulated by his sexual activity.'[20]

For the Indian painter, though, creative activity is directly analogous to what may be called the Yoga of the sexual act. All four stages of creative activity described in the *Yoga Sutras of Patanjali*—selecting or fixing on the object, striving to achieve union, the interval of suspense and the creative climax—are found in the sexual analogy. Several older painters looked back into the years of their lives between twenty and forty—when their sexual activity was at its peak—as their most creative phase. Indian painters believed that there was also a negative side to kama. Sexual activity should not be unrestrained but controlled, two to four times a month, so as to conserve creative energy, which, in the Indian version of sublimation, they directly ascribed to semen.

It is difficult to say how many contemporary Indian artists share with their traditional counterparts the classical Indian view on the nature of the artist who is emotionally balanced, and on artistic creativity which is a matter of connecting with the 'sacred' or a transcendent, spiritual unconscious, as I wish to call it. From my conversations with modern Indian artists, I believe that, although they would reject the classical Indian notion of the artist as balanced and not prone to excess and that they would prefer to embrace the Western stereotype of the 'heroic' artist who is driven by his appetites and who rides an emotional roller coaster, many of them would subscribe to an essentially spiritual or metaphysical view of artistic creativity. In this, they would be nearer to a few Western artists, from Wassily Kandinsky to Francis Bacon, from Joseph Beuys to Damien Hirst, for whom metaphysical questions maintained their significance. Kandinsky, for instance, believed that painting represented 'pure art in the service of the divine.' As is evident from the catalogue of the exhibition Traces du Sacré (Traces of the Sacred), which was on at Centre Pompidou in Paris from 7 May to 11 August, and then moved to Haus der Kunst in Munich, to touch, 'refine and enrich' the 'soul', the 'spirit', has become a central concern for many artists today. They believe that 'the ability to summon a vision of the divine without sentimentality, thus of a secular divine that is embedded in history, is one of the highest skills of the artistic profession'.[21]

The Indian view diverges even more substantially from contemporary Western findings on creativity, not on the role played by unconscious processes but on the nature of the unconscious itself which is outside the reigning scientific paradigm. We now know that perhaps as much as 95 per cent of our mental life is unconscious, hidden from our consciousness which has little or no insight into the motivations which underlie our wishes and actions. Unconscious processes steer our conscious lives, including the creation and appreciation of poetry and art. Modern psychological research has widened the view of unconscious activity, which is much richer and more varied than was postulated by Freud. Of the different types of unconscious processes, one of the more relevant for understanding creativity is the Cognitive Unconscious— unconscious information processing—which involves cognition that has a ready access to both consciousness and what Freud called the Dynamic Unconscious—emotional conflicts, repressed wishes, thoughts and actions.

The classical Indian view on artistic creativity is silent on the kind of unconscious processes that are at the centre of contemporary psychological and neuroscience research. According to this view, creative imagination has access to a transcendent, Spiritual Unconscious which lies in a layer of the mind which is deeper than the strata in which the cognitive, dynamic and other unconscious processes are located. At this deep level, the spiritual unconscious (analogous to Jung's 'primal form'—the profoundest aspect of the psyche) connects with the hidden order of the universe or, in another formulation, is united with the consciousness which animates all existence. In Hindu mystical texts, the attributes of this transcendent-spiritual unconscious are said to be *sat–chit–ananda* (Truth–Being–Delight or Bliss) or *satyam–shivam–sundaram* (Truth–Being–Beauty). Rabindranath

13

Tagore—poet, painter, philosopher and perhaps the greatest multifaceted genius India has produced in the last two hundred years—elaborates:

> Through our sense of truth we realize law in creation, and through our sense of beauty we realize harmony in the universe. When we recognize the law in nature we extend our mastery over physical forces and become powerful; when we recognize the law in our moral nature we attain mastery over self and become free. In like manner, the more we comprehend the harmony in the physical world the more our life shares the gladness of creation, and our expression of beauty in art becomes more truly catholic. As we become conscious of the harmony in our soul, our apprehension of the blissfulness of the spirit of the world becomes universal.[22]

Tagore attributes his own creativity to this transcendent-spiritual unconscious, which he calls the 'One within me'. Adding love to the traditional triad of Truth–Being–Beauty, he says, 'Its creations are a pastime, through which it gives expression to an ideal of unity in its endless show of variety. Such are its pictures, poems, music, in which it finds joy only because they reveal the perfect forms of an inherent unity.'[23] Art, music or poetry which comes into being in response to the fulfilment of the artist's emotional needs is merely constructive, whereas the joy of unity within him, which seeks expression, is creative; artistic creativity is the translation of this truth into our own symbols.

Creative imagination, which 'makes songs not only with words and tunes, lines and colours, but with stones and metals, with ideas and men,' is the common truth both in a human being and in the heart of existence. Since it lies beyond conscious awareness, great artists, writers and music-makers have often felt that their inspiration—the product of this imagination—comes from outside themselves, that it is not self-centred. Considered almost as a truism in India, this has also been the position of many artists and writers in the West in the premodern era although their modern counterparts are reluctant to openly embrace such a 'spiritual' outlook. In his Nobel Prize acceptance speech, Saul Bellow observes, 'The sense of our real powers, powers we seem to derive from the universe itself, also comes and goes. . . . We are reluctant to talk about this because there is nothing we can prove, because our language is inadequate, and because few people are willing to risk talking about it. They would have to say that there is a spirit, and that is taboo.'[24] Premodern geniuses, certainly in India, had no such inhibition. Mirza Ghalib, the great nineteenth-century Urdu poet, could write, '*Aate hain ghaibse ye / mazamiin khyal mein / Ghalib sareer e khama / navaye sarosh hai*' (My thoughts come to me / From somewhere beyond / When Ghalib is attuned / To the music of the stars).

Do emotions, especially those evoked by our conscious and unconscious memories, play no role in the creative works of a genius? Here, Tagore offers a synthesis of sorts between Indian and Western psychological approaches. The consciousness of unity in ourselves, he says, 'becomes prominently distinct when coloured by joy or sorrow, or some other emotion . . . In the creation of art, therefore, the energy of an emotional idea is necessary, as its unity is not like that of a crystal, passive and inert, but actively expressive.'[25] Without the emotional idea, *bhava*, a poem with all its perfection and proportion, rhyme and cadence, would only be a construction; it will not find a synchronous response in the metre of our heartbeats.[26] Creative expressions, then, attain their perfect form through the modulation of emotions.

However, it is undeniable that for Tagore art is more than an expression of emotion, that 'a lyric is indefinably more than the sentiment expressed in it, as a rose is more than its substance.'[27] What makes the ingredients of poetry—perceptions, feelings, language—into a poem is the transformative power of the hidden creative imagination. 'Ideas take shape by some hidden, subtle skill at work within the poet. This creative power is the origin of poetry. Perceptions, feelings, or language, are only raw material. One may be gifted with feeling, a second with language, a third with both; but he, who has as well creative genius, alone is a poet.'[28]

Not only in poetry but also in his life does Tagore see the work of this creative power, the *jibondebata*—literally, god of life. The jibondebata not only weaves fragmentary emotional processes into a continuous significance in art but also, in life, knits up 'all the damage I undergo, piecing it together, shoring it up.'[29] 'An immense memory of a long sequence of existence continuing through this world has gathered round him, and lies in me, in my unconscious,' he writes. 'That is why I feel a kinship of such long standing with the world's flora and fauna. That is why the huge mysterious world does not seem alien and terrible.'[30] The jibondebata not only repairs the damage in the life of a genius but also goes beyond the limits imposed by instincts and narcissism, 'and through deep pain and severance of ties, he is fusing it with what is great and cosmic.'[31] Extraordinary artistic creativity is thus neither a compensation for nor a sublimation of deep pain that reaches back into childhood. The pain only serves to open up a channel in the artist for the flow of the creative power from the spiritual unconscious that both creates and cures.

My own position is sympathetic to that of Tagore although I would emphasize a greater balance between the biological-life historical and the transcendent-spiritual

17

unconscious in the psyche of the artistic genius than he does; in privileging the latter, he may have succumbed to the temptation of underplaying the former. If I may use the Buddhist metaphor of the lotus—a flower opening to light and sun—as the symbol of creativity, symbolizing the transcendent, we also need to remember that the lotus grows in mud, the symbol of the biological-life historical unconscious. The flowering of the lotus needs the mud as much as it needs light and sun, the swirling of drives and emotions in the unconscious as much as the sat–chit–ananda. The mud is not dirt, but, as a mix of the elements of earth and water, it is also the soil of creativity from which the lotus soars above the ground into sunlight. One does not have to subscribe fully to either the sun or mud views on the origins of extraordinary creativity, but one can pay greater attention to the stem, where both the transcendent-spiritual and the biological-emotional flow into each other.

Notes

1. E. Kandel, *The Age of Insight: The Quest to Understand the Unconscious in Art, Mind, and Brain; From Vienna 1900 to the Present* (New York: Random House, 2012). loc 6533.
2. See G. Blamberger, this volume.
3. 'Why is it that all those who have become eminent in philosophy or politics or poetry or the arts are clearly of an atrabilious temperament, and some of them to such an

extent as to be affected by diseases caused by black bile, as is said to have happened to Heracles among the heroes?' (Aristotle, *Problemata* XXX.1 953a, 10–14).

4. G. Holton, *Thematic Origins of Scientific Thought: Kepler to Einstein* (Cambridge, MA: Harvard University Press, 1973), 377.

5. The quotes are from V. Shahly, 'Pregnant with Joy and Sorrow: Creativity, Androgyny, and Manic-Depression,' *The Annual of Psychoanalysis*, 16 (1988): 289–318.

6. Patrick Mahony, in an interview with the author, 4 July 2012.

7. Shahly, 313.

8. See S.K. De, *History of Sanskrit Poetics*, vol. 2 (Kolkata: Firma K.L.P., 1976) 39.

9. Beginning with Freud, the psychoanalytic literature on the creative process and the creative person is vast. Some of the more recent books are: G. Hagman, *The Artist's Mind: A Psychoanalytic Perspective on Creativity, Modern Art and Modern Artists* (London and New York: Routledge, 2010); J. Oremland, *The Origins and Psychodynamics of Creativity: A Psychoanalytic Perspective* (University of Michigan: International Universities Press, 1997).

10. V.S. Ramachandran and W. Hirstein, 'The Science of Art: A Neurological Theory of Aesthetic Experience,' *Journal of Consciousness Studies* 6, no. 6–7 (1999):15–51; V.S. Ramachandran and E.M. Hubbard, 'Synaesthesia: A Window into Perception, Thought and Language,' *Journal of Consciousness Studies* 8, no. 12 (2001): 3–34.

11. See M. Boden, 'Creativity as a Neuroscientific Mystery', this volume.

12. H. Gardner, *Creating Minds. An Anatomy of Creativity Seen through the Eyes of Freud, Einstein, Picasso, Stravinsky, Eliot, Graham, and Ghandi* (New York: The Perseus Books Group), 36.

13. A. Coomaraswamy, *The Dance of Shiva* (Delhi: Manohar, 2009), 26.

14. A. Coomaraswamy, *Introduction to Indian Art* (Delhi: Munshiram Manoharlal, 1966), 80.

15. R. Maduro, *Artistic Creativity in a Brahmin Painter Community* (Berkeley, CA: Center for South and Southeast Asia Studies, 1976).

16. Maduro, 141.

17. S. Freud (1928), 'Dostoevsky and Parricide,' in *The Standard Edition of the Complete Psycological Works of Sigmund Freud*, ed. J. Strachey, vol. 21, 1952–61 (London: Hogarth Press), 177.

18. Maduro, 136.

19. Maduro, 136.

20. S. Freud (1908), 'Civilized Sexual Morality and Modern Nervousness,' in *The Standard Edition of the Complete Psycological Works of Sigmund Freud*, ed. J. Strachey, vol. 9, 1952–61 (London: Hogarth Press), 197.

21. J. Kounellis, *Catalogue Traces du Sacré.*

22. R. Tagore, 'The Realisation of Beauty,' in *Sadhana: the Realisation of Life* (London: Macmilan, 1913). For Tagore, 'truth' is knowing things in their relation to the universe. Truth consists not of facts, but lies in the harmony of facts.

23. *Creative Unity*, VI. Although Tagore's views on artistic creativity will find some support in the writings of a few Western philosophers, such as Gadamer, Heidegger and Maritan, I can think of only one psychoanalyst, R.D. Chessick (2005), who will find them congenial to his own thought. See R.D. Chessick, 'What Grounds Creativity?' *Journal of the American Academy of Psychoanalysis* 33 (2005): 7–28.

24. Cited in J.A. Knight, 'The Spiritual as a Creative Force in the Person,' *Journal of the American Academy of Psychoanalysis* 15 (1987): 365.

25. Tagore, *Creative Unity*, 34.

26. Tagore, *Creative Unity*, 35.

27. Tagore, *Creative Unity*, 36.

28. Letter to Indira Devi, 10 July 1893.

29. Tagore, *Of Myself: Atma Parichay*, 3.

30. Tagore, *Of Myself: Atma Parichay*, 4–5.

31. Tagore, *Of Myself: Atma Parichay*, 4.

Creativity as Experience and Process:
On Myths and New Concepts of Creativity

Günter Blamberger

Le baiser de la muse is the title of one of Cézanne's first paintings, probably from 1859–60. It depicts a poet in his nightly retreat, with his eyes closed and his head resting on his hand—the typical attitude of the melancholic—an angel standing behind him, gently kissing him on the forehead. Here, the poet's inspiration is depicted as a transpersonal, divinatory gift, the Christian angel replacing the Greek muse. I first saw this painting in the mid-1980s at Musée Granet in Aix-en-Provence, and it induced me to work on the secret of the creative, which became the title of a book, published in 1991.[1] I found the painting fascinating for several reasons. It is obvious that Cézanne does not owe its conception to a muse, in that it is just the copy of a painting made by the now-forgotten academic painter, Félix Nicolas Frillié, two years earlier, in 1857. The original and the copy are now arranged side by side in the museum and seemingly offer an evident demonstration of the Greek myth that assigns no muse to painting, because painting needs no divine inspiration since it is just a craft, learnable by copying reality or models. The real scandalon, here, is that Cézanne paints a wholly uninspired picture about inspiration; uninspired for two reasons: firstly because it is a mere copy, and secondly because he proves incapable of replacing the old topos of transpersonal, divine ability of the poet by a muse with a contemporary figure, showing the poet as the responsible subject of his artefacts.

As his letters to Zola prove, Cézanne no longer believed in the divine blessing of the poet. Cézanne's interpreters, then, without further ado, clipped the angel's wings and suspected the muse to be his *hypothétique maîtresse* or even his mother, who treasured *Le baiser de la muse*, given to her as a present, for the rest of her life. Thanks to Rilke's letter to his wife Clara, written in Paris 1907, we know better: Cézanne did not even have the time to attend his mother's funeral, finding himself 'sur le motif'.[2] Rilke only mentions this *skandalon* in order to characterize Cézanne as an obsessive worker who did not require any such moments of wondrous inspiration, but, instead, intently painted the same landscape over and over again—the mountains of Sainte-Victoire, near Aix.

Fig. 1. *Le baiser de la muse*, by Paul Cézanne[3]

Cézanne's contemporary Nietzsche, notes in the chapter, 'From the Soul of Artists and Writers', of his book *Human, All Too Human: A Book for Free Spirits* (1878): 'All of the Greats were great workers', debunking the 'belief in inspiration' as an 'all too human' illusion, all too readily welcomed by both artists and the public. A welcome illusion since, on the

25

one hand, the assumption of a divine blessing multiplies the artist's aura, while, on the other hand, it shields the audience from any self-criticism. After all, nobody must compare himself to a genius, who owes his masterpiece to divine vocation and not his individual efforts.[4]

Fig. 2. *Melencolia I*, by Albrecht Dürer[5]

Nietzsche is a sceptical moralist, who practises the art of disillusion in a godless world. On the other hand, in the reproduction of Frillić's painting, Cézanne proves to be a rather late romantic, the subtitle of his copy being *Le rêve du poète*. It maintains the anachronistic illusion of a transpersonal blessing, but only in the form of possibility, in the conjunctive mood of a dream. His depiction of the muse's kiss could therefore just as well be read as a modern poet's dream of the return of a divine blessing and the return of the Absolute, in the face of the limitations of modern genius in its own subjectivity. This interpretation is possible because, in Cézanne's painting, the old motif of the transpersonal inspiration by a muse interferes with the motif of the modern genius's melancholy. This motif is familiar to us, for instance, from Dürer's engraving, *Melencolia I*, from 1514—the image of a sad thinker, personified by a most earthly, that is, a heavy, not airy, angel. He has taken the circle from the hands of God—the original builder of the world—in order to measure and rebuild the world on his own. Against the wall of a new building—only a cottage—leans a ladder, and the self-appointed world architect is sitting on a stone bench with his head resting heavily on his hand, paralysed by doubt and despair. Here, Dürer combines the deadly sins, pride and sloth, *superbia* and *acedia*, known from scholastic theology with the medical and philosophical

27

notions of the advantages and risks of melancholy, the predominance of black bile within the system of humours prominent since Aristotle's *Problemata Physica* XXX, 1. According to Aristotle or, rather, to Theophrastus, 'all those who become eminent in philosophy or politics or poetry or the arts' are melancholics. Due to temperature changes of the black bile, they are multi-tempered, thereby transcending 'the mundane order of the majority of people'. At the same time, however, they are faced with the risk of a fall from the exceptional state of the genius to the pathological states of manic or depressive illness, accompanied by doubts about the mythical world order as well as exclusion from the community.[6]

Dürer's engraving, which so impressively unifies melancholy and ingenuity, in the following ages becomes a genius-badge, a passport portrait for intellectuals. There is a photograph of Walter Benjamin, taken by Gisèle Freund in 1938, showing the impact of a humour such as the black bile, which in reality does not exist. Cézanne's painting in the tradition of Dürer's engraving could thus perhaps be seen as a continuation of the topos of the melancholy-heroic genius, of its transcendental homelessness and of the dream of a return of the absolute in a renewed 'destiny to a totality' (Georg Lukács). Of course, this is highly speculative and rather recalls Thomas

Mann's artist's metaphysics in his *Doktor Faustus* novel, in which the composer Adrian Leverkühn, who has Dürer's melancholy-engraving hanging above his piano, makes a pact with the devil in order to overcome the incidence of subjectivity.

Fig. 3. Walter Benjamin, 1938

Source: Photo Gisèle Freund/IMEC/Fonds/MCC

To come back to the nineteenth century, Cézanne's painting is an example of the hopeless aporias and myths which even artists renew when they question the personal origin of the creative. Poets share this helplessness and, in line with them, scholars of creativity studies too, in exploring and relying on biographies of poets and artists, as the first part of my essay will show, analysing the historical and systematical background. In the second part, I will try to break this vicious circle by suggesting a reflection on creativity as experience and process, following Heinrich von Kleist's essay, *On the Gradual Production of Thoughts whilst Speaking*. In the third part, finally, I will map out a few of the consequences of the current departure from the conception of genius which has been prominent in Western culture since the eighteenth century.

I. Aporias and myths

The word 'school' derives from the Greek *scholé*, which originally meant 'leisure' and addressed the privilege of aristocrats who were exempt from doing hard work and who were free to pursue philosophical, scientific and artistic interests. Only leisure can, if at all, ever be a sufficient condition for creativity—a dream still maintained by the anti-authoritarian pedagogy of the second half of the twentieth century. What is perhaps more realistic is the proverb 'Necessity is the mother of invention'. Necessity is—and this is not a play with semantics, but rather a general law of evolution—the necessary condition for creativity. Within the history of science, the emergence of creativity studies itself is an example of the correlation between creativity and crisis. The term 'creativity' became a scientific concept in the 1950s. It was coined by the American military psychologist, Joy Paul Guilford, who was the first to develop conceptions and methods of tests for the differentiation between divergent and convergent thinkers, incorporating historical testimonies of creativity from poets, artists and scientists. A catalyst for the American research on creativity was the Sputnik crisis, the fear of being technologically inferior to Soviet Russia. Progress appeared to be halted, and Germany, like Europe, figured as a political and cultural waiting room, hesitant of a future-oriented thinking and acting. Paradoxically, the basic term 'creativity' and its associated notes of 'innovation', 'future of the knowledge society', 'elite' and 'excellence' have, in the past years, been in use in Germany as well.

Great importance is attached to creativity in the arts, in science, technology and the media, and is being socially decorated with private or public reputation as well as with numerous awards. On the other side, there is a strange reluctance on the part of science to analyse creativity. The question of creativity in psychology—the 'mother discipline' of creativity studies—as in all other fields concerned with the emergence of the new, is not a central concern, but marginalized. What is missing is an integrative creatology that could help answer the interdisciplinary question of how 'newness' enters the world; as a cooperation of art and media studies, philosophy, psychology, sociology, neurobiology, evolutionary research, etc. Mihaly Csikszentmihalyi has called for the foundation of such an integrative creatology in his 1996 book *Creativity*.[7] In vain, as far as I know. However, I would be glad to be proven wrong.

Why is it so? This is my first question. I suggest that it is because creativity studies have always set wrong priorities in focusing on the question of the personal origin of creativity, leading to hopeless aporias and reproducing myths of the creative. There are both historical and systematic reasons for this. The systematic error first: there appears to be a consensus in creativity studies that creativity is supposed to imply not only a new combination of old elements, but also the creation of fundamentally new ones. By definition, then, creative processes cannot be reduced to a given set of antecedents and their principles and rules; they are not logically or causally deducible from existing, initial elements and therefore not predictable. This is the main reason for the failure of attempts to provide a scientific explanation when addressing the personal origin of creativity.

The German philosopher, Immanuel Kant, was aware of the ultimate hopelessness of explaining the personal origin of creativity. In his *Critique of Judgment*, first published in 1790, Kant noted that the origin of creativity is unknown to the creative person and, accordingly, it 'cannot describe or indicate scientifically how it brings about its products . . . Hence the author of a product for which he is indebted to his genius does not himself know how he has come by his ideas; and he has not the power . . . to communicate it to others in precepts that will enable them to produce similar products.'[8] An analysis of literary or artistic depictions of creativity confirms this notion: from an internal author's view, even more so from an external scientist's view, scientific attempts to explain the origin of creativity fail, as Kant reluctantly had to confess in his *Anthropology from a Pragmatic Point of View* (1798). He identified the ability of the genius as an invisibility of a cause to an impact. According to Kant, the true cause for creation is beyond all rational analysis.

What, then, can be scientifically said concerning creativity? Since Kant took the *ingenium*—the aptitude or giftedness—to be as *ineffabile*, that is, incomparable, as the individual who bore it, he abandoned the question about the originality of a genius and changed his view. Kant suggested considering the question of creativity not as about the 'origin of production', but as about the 'produced work', about whose exceptionality the community of readers has formed an opinion. In his *Critique of Judgment* Kant noted: '*Genius* is the talent (or natural gift) which gives the rule to Art' and 'the rule must be abstracted from the fact, i.e. from the product'.[9] The genius thus becomes recognizable only through his work. Kant's shift from the side of production to that of reception is reasonable and, to some extent, it is an escape from seemingly unanswerable to seemingly more easily answerable questions.

When attempts at a scientific explanation fail, it seems natural to seek salvation in anachronistic myths of the creative. Or, in other words, Kant's attempt to define creativity as the creation of the new without presuppositions is aporetic in sticking to the myth of the *creatio ex nihilo*— the divine creation out of nothing at the beginning of the Bible—which has become a commonplace in descriptions of human creativity in biographies and autobiographies of artists, poets, scholars, etc., since the eighteenth century. A good example of this can be found in more recent literary history, in a 1965 poem by the Romanian poet,

Marin Sorescu, on Shakespeare, translated into English by
Michael Hamburger:

Shakespeare

Shakespeare created the world in seven days.

On the first day he made the sky and the mountains and
    the ravines of the soul.
On the second day he made the rivers, the seas, the
    oceans as well as
the other feelings and
gave them to Hamlet, to Julius Caesar, to Cleopatra,
    Ophelia,
Othello and others, to
reign over them with their children and later descendants
for ever and ever.

On the third day he summoned the whole of humanity
to teach them the diverse tastes:
the taste of happiness, that of love, the taste
of despair, of jealousy, fame etc.,
till there were none left to distribute. But then
a few people came who were late.
Sorry for them, the creator patted their heads and
    informed them
there was nothing left for them save

to become literary critics and
debunk his work.

The fourth and fifth days he reserved for laughter, gave
the clowns a free hand, allowed them
to turn somersaults and so provided amusement for
kings and emperors and other unfortunate persons.
On the sixth day he dealt with administrative problems:
he set up a storm
and taught King Lear
how to wear a crown of straw.

There was some waste matter, too, from creation, and
    out of this
he made Richard III.
On the seventh day he made sure that nothing was left
    undone.
Already theatre managers had plastered
the whole world with their playbills, and
Shakespeare thought that after so much hard work
he deserved to see a performance;
but meanwhile, because he felt so excessively drowsy,
he lay down to take
forty winks of death.[10]

As a 'literary critic' I stop here, but not without
assuring you that I am not a polemic and I only work

on authors whose work I love. This is the case with Sorescu's poem, which quotes the Bible. The history of creation in the Bible is unique in its separating theogony and cosmogony. In other mythological texts, God or gods and the world come into being at the same time. In the Bible, the secret of creation, through God's absolute transcendence, becomes the secret of the creator, who is without presupposition and who alone can create the complete new. God's doing has a post-history, but not a pre-history. This is his wonder and it distinguishes his form of creative power from that of man. Yet the topos of creatio ex nihilo is still the most cited in descriptions and self-description of artistic creation processes and, again, effectively underlines Kant's or Joy Paul Guilford's definition of creative man, establishing the nearly unapproachable secret of creativity.

This aporia is not only a system error in defining creativity; it also has a historical place. It is not by chance that I cited the Shakespeare poem. In the eighteenth century, Shakespeare was held as a role model for the autonomy of creative man. One cannot think of the genius era without referring to him. One of the most influential concepts of a Western theory of art has undoubtedly been a concept of creativity intrinsically linked to the philosophy of the subject and centred in the notion of an individual creator as the origin of all art.

Shaftesbury proclaimed the genius, claimed Shakespeare as 'a second *Maker*: a just PROMETHEUS, under JOVE' (under Jupiter).[11] Goethe's hymn, *Prometheus*, defiantly reads towards the end: 'Here I sit, form human beings, /After my image; /A race that will be equal to me'.[12] Thus do Shaftesbury and Goethe remain tied to divinity as the matrix of human creation. The pathos of autonomy in Shaftesbury, Goethe and many others in the eighteenth century is a mere ironic play to Sorescu, two centuries later. Still, altogether, they appear helpless in trying to base the origin of human creativity in human nature.

One of the big unsettling questions which have been passed on from the eighteenth century to the following centuries is the question of the genealogical authority of the creative subject and the describability of a creative origin. The genius aesthetic of the eighteenth century had shaken faith in inspiration as a divine gift, but it had been unable to solve the original problem. Divine creatorship had been far more familiar, but human creatorship had, as early as in the art philosophies of the late-eighteenth and early-nineteenth centuries, proven inconceivable. Since the personal origin of creativity marks such a crucial point of difficulty, the risk involved in producing legends and myths in the biographies of poets and artists is obvious. Are the scientists' reports of inspiration more reliable? I'm afraid not. I need only remind you of the chemist August

Kekulé, who, in 1865, allegedly conceived of the idea of Benzene's ring structure of six carbon atoms through a dream that he had of a snake biting its tail. Obviously a Bible quote, alluding to the serpent in Paradise and the Fall of man. There is always a likelihood of being met with a mystification of the genius for the purpose of making the extraordinary seemingly comprehensible to the ordinary reader.

After all these examples of mystification and futility, it is time to search for some way out of this hopeless problem of the individual origin of creativity.

Modern creativity studies distinguish between four respects of inquiry: 'person', 'product', 'process' and 'press'. 'Press' means the social conditions of creativity. As mentioned, Kant shifts his analytical focus from 'person' to 'product' and concerns himself with the conditions of the audience's acceptance of genius works. What I find to be more thrilling is Kleist's thoughts on creativity which, in contrast, are concerned with neither the individual origin of production nor the produced work. He is interested in 'process' and 'press'. This becomes particularly clear in an essay which, even today, marks a challenge to creativity studies—a groundbreaking essay titled On the Gradual Formation of Thoughts while Speaking, written in Königsberg in 1805–1806.

II. Creativity as experience and process

Kleist's essay starts out harmlessly, by proposing the 'rule' of prudence which states that, like appetite, which comes with eating, thoughts come in the process of speaking. A series of quite heterogeneous case studies illustrates this claim. What they have in common is that, following an uncertain beginning or silence, the gradual formation of thoughts while speaking stages a test of creativity which features an agonal structure in the communication of subject and observer. Evidently, Kleist considers aggression to be a catalyst of creativity, whether it is scholarly, artistic or political. In each case, the aggression is directed towards an opponent embodying real or symbolic social institutions that restrain the individual's self-development. In the first case, Kleist, becoming 'excite[d]' while solving a mathematical problem, outtalks his peaceful, quiet sister 'like a general' [12] as if performing an urgent act of self-assertion against a representative of familial determination. The second case sees Molière prevail over his maidservant who—as an imaginary opponent—anticipates the literary audience's judgement of his emerging drama. The third case deals with political liberation attempts, with the onset of the French Revolution in Mirabeau's speech of June 1789, in which he defies Louis XVI's orders to disband the National Assembly. The fourth case recounts La Fontaine's fable, *Les animaux malades de la peste*. The lion, the king of animals, looking for someone to blame for the outbreak of the plague, sentences the fox, who is guilty of the worst sins, to death. The lion represents the constraining power of the naturally strongest, but the fox succeeds in saving his neck by an artful speech. Kleist's final example is a university examination. The test of creativity fails here, because the examiner doesn't allow for any rivalry with the examinee, expecting only his own echo and not the finalist's 'peculiar sound'.

Nothing new can come of mere imitation. In regard to a history of literature and of mentalities, Kleist's images of creativity demonstrate his association with the artistic debate of the seventeenth and eighteenth centuries: the *querelle des Anciens et des Modernes* at the Académie française in 1687, the famous quarrel about the merits of contemporary culture compared to those of the ancient, as well as its continuation in the genius discourse of European enlightenment. Here, the idea of a competition between the generations becomes prominent, the necessary rebellion of the new against the old, the notion of nonconformity as a precondition for originality. Edward Young's *Conjectures on Original Composition* (published 1759) marks a model for the rebellious German authors of Sturm und Drang (storm and stress), in that it once again shakes the three main pillars of the older literary and arts theory—the centuries-old conviction that human creativity is a *trias* of ingenium (as divine inspiration); *ars* (as a technical mastery of the rules of art); and *doctrina* (as scholarly knowledge). Now ars and doctrina became less important, and ingenium was defined as an individual talent, not a divine one. According to Young, '[Nature] brings us into the world all *Originals*: No two faces, no two minds, are just alike; but all bear Nature's evident mark of Separation on them. Born *Originals*, how comes it to pass that we die *Copies*? That meddling Ape *Imitation* . . . snatches the Pen, and blots out nature's mark of Separation, cancels her kind intention, destroys all mental Individuality' To Young, therefore, the pattern of genius is the pattern of his individuality which is to be recognized and reproduced— in Kleist's words, in one's own 'peculiar sound'. There we have it again: Young's definition of genius is aporetic, insofar as *individuum* and ingenium become incomparable. Today, what remains from Young's *Conjectures* is a negative foundation of genius, found in his suggestion according to which genius should leave the 'beaten, the main path' of many in order to follow his own 'path' and then trust in chance or in competition with a rival. Originality— to Young—is what '[c]hance often discovers' or a 'noble stroke of emulation from another's glory . . .'

Kleist himself doesn't seem to present a great deal of originality in marking creativity as a critical test of the enforcement of the creative's peculiarity and extraordinariness. He is, however, more radical than Young, and more radical than the aesthetic philosophies of German idealism. In Friedrich Schiller's conception of aesthetic education, for example, the precondition for autonomy of the mind is the division of its sphere, separating art from 'practical life'. In his essay, *On the Gradual Formation of Thoughts while Speaking*, however, Kleist does not allow for this playful exit strategy. The social institutions, in effect, are the field in which one has to prove one's ability to help himself to the creative spirit, enabling empowerment by commanding or destroying the powers that restrain the individual's self-development. Kleist is an aristocrat and former warrior, sometimes at a great distance from German idealism. The constitution of the genius is no longer tied to a moral legitimation in Kleist's examples. Even the poets of the genius era of storm and stress had rebelled against authority in the name of heart, reason and morality. In Kleist's essay, there is no mention of the substance of formatted thoughts, nor does creativity play a part in the education of mankind, as it does in idealism. The fox in Kleist's version of La Fontaine's fable does not want to stop the lion's plan for a sacrifice. His rhetoric does not aim at achieving the lion's aesthetic education. He just saves himself with the destructive flash inspiration to point out another candidate for death amidst his listeners: the innocent donkey.

Kleist's essay *On the Gradual Formation of Thoughts while Speaking* does not reveal much about the talent of the creative, the phases of creative thinking and the final product—the mathematical, political or literary idea. From a contemporary point of view, it could be said that, first, he works like a psychologist, defining aggression, the struggle for singularity and autonomy 'within' and 'against' social institutions as catalysts for the process of creativity—beyond considering the substances of the produced ideas. Second, he works like a media theorist and cognitive scientist. And this is the actual sensation and groundbreaking dimension in his doctrine of creativity, whose surprise is already found in its title: thoughts are produced gradually while speaking, that is, in and through their medium. Kleist thus reverses the basic assumption of traditional rhetoric, according to which thinking precedes speaking, with the speaker expanding on a previously formed thought in controlled and effective speech. According to Kleist, on the contrary, thoughts which are formed gradually while speaking owe themselves to the 'obstinacy of the medium language'. They are not transcendent of language, but exclusively pertaining to language.

Consequently, the creative process is neither a mere translation from an internal language of the brain—a language of internal thoughts—nor a translation from the external world in the sense of reproduction or mimesis. Creativity, in Kleist, does not appear as the reproduction of previously made or thought experience, but a mode of experience within the medium itself, 'which will shape confused ideas into complete clarity'. In Latin terms, a *perceptio confusa* transforms itself into a *perceptio distincta* by way of speech and potentially disturbing and disrupting objections to it. Let me quote the passage from the above essay:

> But because I do have some dim conception at the outset, one distantly related to what I am looking for, if I boldly make a start with that, my mind, even as my speech proceeds, under the necessity of finding an end for that beginning, will shape my first confused idea into complete clarity so that, to my amazement, understanding is arrived at as the sentence ends. I put in a few unarticulated sounds, dwell lengthily on the conjunctions, perhaps make use of apposition where it is not necessary, and have recourse to other tricks which will spin out my speech, all to gain time for the fabrication of my idea in the workshop of the mind. And in this process nothing helps me more than if my sister makes a move suggesting she wishes to interrupt; for such an attempt from outside to wrest speech from its grasp still further excites my already hard-worked mind and, like a general when circumstances press, its powers are raised a further degree.

Order from noise is the calculus. The prudence rule is: Submit to the figures of regulation of the medium, the speech itself; try to act calmly without knowing the direction of your actions. The situation, then, is paradoxical, the language–action recursive: By means of the still-unstructured speech, the speaker gains time for distinguishing thoughts that are to be found only in hearing himself speak, which he does by making use of the formational features of the medium. The medium—in this case, speech—paradoxically facilitates creativity in the obstructiveness and peculiarity of its semantic, syntactical and pragmatic uses and restrictions.

According to Kleist, the trigger of ideas is the medium of expression. There is no consciousness outside of language; it structures and generates itself within language. The medium is always prior to consciousness. Kleist contradicts the notion of creativity as an ingenious subject's independent cognitive capacity prior to all activity, deliberately occupying any one medium for the purpose of its actualization. For him, creativity is knowledge of experience which is only generated *in action*. In contrast to the genius aesthetic, Kleist provocatively notes: 'For it is not we who *know*. It is a certain *state of us* that *knows*.' For him, creativity is by no means a calculable process in the sense of a transformation of knowledge and schemes into action, but a mode of experience: in speaking and speaking on as well as in writing and writing on, in the working processes of a painter or a sculptor as well as in those of a composer. *Art as experience* of a shared agency between artist and medium, or material, artist and imaginary or real observers. The creative person is part of a test arrangement, there is no externality to creative experiments and, according to Kleist's case studies again, those experiments are most rewarding of innovation, in which the unforeseen takes place, and disturbances interrupt the creative process. Creativity always requires a readiness to assume risks, particularly in understanding the constructive qualities of disturbances and a readiness to, in a sense, be 'overwritten' by the medium or the observer. Kleist agrees that necessity is the mother of invention or, with the German sociologist, Niklas Luhmann: Creativity is about 'the use of contingencies for the purpose of building structures.' Kleist's action- and media-theoretical conception of creativity sounds very modern. It is a challenge to date, to a generation living in a media age, to a generation of precarity which is unable to follow life plans, but can only ever conceive temporary projects.

III. Farewell to Genius: Views on new concepts of creativity

'Farewell to Genius' is the title of the third part of my talk, in which I will outline my views on contemporary creativity studies. I will, again, set out with two examples. The first is from Peter Shaffer's play *Amadeus*, so successfully made into a film by Milos Forman. It is about the rivalry between the composers Mozart and Salieri. At the beginning we see—you might remember the play or the film—Salieri attending a concert which Mozart is to conduct, hosted by the archbishop of Salzburg. Salieri does not know his famous competitor and searches through all the rooms of the palace for a face showing the unmistakable mark of genius, the sign of divine chosenness. What he finds, instead, is— in Salieri's words—'a performing monkey', rolling on the floor with Constanze and finding great pleasure in scatology, as in 'kiss my arse', which he can spell forward and backward. Salieri is shocked: 'Why? Why would God choose an obscene child to be His instrument? It was not to be believed!' Mozart, on the other hand, is surprised that Salieri wants to speak with God's voice— his, Mozart's, method of composition works differently. Mozart says: 'I tell you I want to write a finale lasting half an hour! A quartet becoming a quintet becoming a sextet. On and on, wider and wider—all sounds multiplying and rising together—and the together creating a sound entirely new! . . . I bet you that's how God hears the world: millions of sounds ascending at once and mixing in His ear to become an unending music, unimaginable to us! That's our job, we composers: to combine the inner minds of him and him and him and her and her—the thoughts of chambermaids and Court Composers—and turn the audience into God.'

Not with only one voice, let alone with the voice of God, like Salieri, does Mozart want to *speak*, but with many voices, with the voices of the people that God *hears*. According to Shaffer, Mozart's art is based on multi-voicedness, polyphony in a verbal, not musical-theoretical meaning. Mozart quotes and transforms the musical tradition, wishing to be neither God nor a genius as 'second maker under Jove'. Not to mention Goethe's Faust or Thomas Mann's Adrian Leverkühn, who make pacts with the devil, in order to perceive and then to announce, 'whatever holds / The world together in its inmost folds'.

A second example, Bertolt Brecht's story, *Originality*, from *Stories of Mr Keuner*: 'Nowadays', complains Mr K., 'there are innumerable people who boast in public that they are able to write great books all by themselves, and this meets with general approval. When he was already in the prime of life, the Chinese philosopher, Chuang-tzu, composed a book of 100,000 words, nine-tenths of which consisted of quotations. Such books can no longer be written here and now, because the wit is lacking. As a result, ideas are only produced in one's own workshop, and anyone who does not manage enough of them thinks himself lazy. Admittedly, there is then not a single idea that could be adopted or a single formulation of an idea that could be quoted. How little all of them need for their activity! A pen and some paper are the only things they are able to show! And without any help, with only the scant material that anyone can carry in his hands, they erect their cottages! The largest buildings they know are those a single man is capable of constructing!'

By the way, Brecht polemizes against a typically German favourite: the Bildungsroman—a literary form unknown to other nations. Ever since Goethe's *Wilhelm Meister*, young poets have been writing *Bildungs-* or *Entwicklungsromane* as an expression of a singular, unique, distinctive, unmistakable originality. In Asia, this would be unthinkable, as even the biographies of celebrated women or men deal with the disappearance of personal history into contemporary history. The concept of genius, says Brecht, is historically passé; it may have held up for 200 years in Western culture. In Eastern culture, it never held in the first place, and a closer look reveals the necessary misery of a pure self-sense, of a focus on mere individual expression, private experiences and a distinct voice in comparison to the multi-voicedness and polyphony, the relational sense of what Western poetics of premodern centuries called *esprit*, wit or *Witz*. In this sense, it was not the private that was communicated, but the commonly shared. 'Original composition' in premodern, pre-individual eras was a matter of ars and doctrina, the mastery of rules of art, subjects and motifs. According to Brecht, it should be the same in post-individual eras.

Brecht, Shaffer: these are only two examples of many. In the wake of the avant-gardes of the twentieth century, the concept of genius is dismissed by authors and artists alike. It is time that the research on creativity followed their example. That is why my first proposition is:

Proposition 1: A paradigm shift in Western creativity studies is necessary— a departure from the concept of genius and from the focus on singular creatorship.

I must stress that I'm referring to Western culture, since the concept of genius has not played a role in any other culture. Please correct me if I'm wrong. In Asian culture, for instance, a conception of mastery to me seems central, of a respectful imitation and gradual improvement of felicitous models. This is a notion also dominant in Western culture prior to the genius era; the definition of creativity as an ability that requires education and formation and is not the mere imprint of only one's own originality. Shaffer's interpretation of Mozart as a polyphonic composer in the sense of Bakthin citing and varying the musical tradition is correct. And Shakespeare—role model of the genius era—was, in fact, a playwright who developed his plays with and within his theatre company. His plays, apparently, owe their richness not to his own originality, but to a collective creativity. For ideological reasons of a rebellion against all authorities, the genius era shifted the origin of creativity from the factor *studium* (as social action, as the practice of available knowledge) to the factor ingenium (as a personal giftedness preceding all creative activity), thereby only just making the 'ingenium' as incomparable and unique as the 'individuum'.

The crucial point, however, is this: the psychology of creativity as the master discipline of creativity studies has, since the 1950s, simply upheld these aporetic appointments of genius, which had once been tied to aesthetic discourses from the eighteenth to the twentieth century, and transferred them to other fields of activity outside the arts. It has continued to work with a conception of singular creatorship. Paradoxically, the test methods— with the help of which one aimed to find divergent thinkers for a competitive economy and science— simultaneously de-individualized again the concept of creativity. Guilford, for instance, developed test methods for the appointment of creative key qualifications. He named four: fluency, flexibility, originality and elaboration. The fluency factor refers to the number of ideas generated; the flexibility factor refers to their qualitative variety; the originality factor refers to the number of unusual ideas compared to the other answers of a test group; and the elaboration factor refers to the ability to expand the ideas to a detailed plan. The special qualities of creativity are thus detached from the individual history of development, and the creative personality is regarded rather as a carrier than a responsible subject of creative forces, the application of which, likewise, is no longer aimed mainly at the generation of singularity and autonomy, as it was in the genius era. A person's creative potential is instrumentalized for the creation of innovative products. The only remaining common notion between the new conception of creativity and the idea of genius is that of a person's creative potential preceding all creative activity. The auratic concept of genius, however, is devaluated, hollowed out and universalized. Therefore, it should not come as a surprise that, in 1988, a book with the title *Creativity: An Obsolete Concept* was published in Germany, in which Niklas Luhmann described creativity as 'democratically deformed ingenuity'. My position, however, is that it is not the term creativity that is to be dismissed, but the one-sided focus on the factor of the 'creative person' in the research on creativity.

Proposition 2: Creativity can no longer refer to the individual, if a theory of creativity is to meet with the requirements of today's creative practices, which are mostly processes based on a division of labour within collective and dynamic networks.

In new media, in management, in the research labs of industries and universities, individual processes of creation are currently the exception rather than the rule. In most workplaces today, creativity is a division of labour which is functionally and personally differentiated and dependent on the systemic conditions of the field of work as well as the media of expression and their obstinacy, that is, their particularity. Creativity is negotiated in a complicated architecture of networks, in a process of the shared agency of humans, gadgets and other apparatuses. The creative process of the different actors is not to be thought as additive, in the sense of an assembly line, but rather in the sense of overwriting each other—a constant movement of translation—and of a shifting of sense in the given fields, medial formats, appliances. This is best explained using the example of film production.

Let us assume that an actor reads a script in which, in grave sentences, he is to be assigned the role of a melancholic genius, and imagines an enactment, a staging for it. According to Pier Paolo Pasolini, the structure of a script is a 'structure wanting to be another structure'. The fixed literal sentences must be able to be embodied in oral language, in facial expressions, gestures and movement. But can there be a smooth transition between the literal sentences of the script and the images of the film? Is there a 'logic of in-between'? Naïve screenwriters attempt to fix this transitory logic by adding suggestions for enacting to the dialogues in the script as a subtext. Nothing angers actors, directors, costume designers, set designers and other 'creatives' involved in the collective process of the production of a film more than this. What is hereby disregarded is the peculiarity of the cinematic image towards the text as well as the circumstance that there can at the most be an analogous, never a causal, relation between the sentences in a script and the images in a film. The sentence 'I am so melancholic today' may be represented by black clothes, a walk in a foggy winter scene, head bent forward or the construction of a bleak apartment. Between text and cinematic image there can be no linear translation, no continuous transition or logical transfer from one medium to the other; in actuality, it is a leap from one medium to the other, at the postulate of a purely functional analogy in mood. In the transition of a script into a film, the screenwriter loses his (or her) authority. It is handed over to costume designers, directors of photography, set designers, whose aesthetics, in turn, may be wholly different from those of the writer. The creativity of a set designer, for instance, in the exchange of fragmented gazes, close-ups and distance shots, follows a supplementary logic. The set designer can turn an empty school gym into a hospital or university by a few requisites later filmed in isolation. The creativity of a make-up artist, in contrast, follows a micro-logic of the concrete and small—every curl of hair becomes the interpretation of a character.

In principle, film is produced in a shared agency, that is, negotiated between agents taking different roles of action, sequentially operating different media of expression and—through this—overwriting each other. Let us now assume that the film is complete, a scene just as melancholy as the actor, the set designer and the film director had wished it to be, but the film director—already involved in the next project—is unable to be there for post-production. As you know, in post-production, the cutter brings the film to completion by choosing from among the provided takes, each assembled from many shots. The cutter, being afforded only a couple of seconds per scene, is unable to incorporate all images. What if, instead of a close-up of the actor's melancholy expression, he chooses the reverse shot, the loving look of the dialogue partner! What if he doesn't choose the distance shot that emphasizes the claustrophobia of the room—as the set designer had envisioned—but the medium long shot of both dialogue partners, comfortable on a cosy sofa! The cutter passes the final cut to the film composer who now scores the scene with cheerful music. The result of it all? Actors, set designer and film director become violently angry at the performance of the final approval.

The conclusion of this would be that, potentially, not only in film but also in all cooperative processes of creation, any agent and any medium of expression can overwrite any other agent and any other medium. Agency oscillates and sense may always shift. Instead of ingenious 'individuals', one should, then, assume *dividuals* in the creative process, since team creativity is determined by polar relations between interacting persons whose personal potential is always influenced by that of the others. The agents develop differences, yet they are, at the same time, always inseparably connected. One's weakness may, gradually, become another's strength, and vice versa. In other words, in the making of a film, all persons involved are sometimes active agents and sometimes overwritten passive patients of actions. A subject-oriented concept of action—such as the one we find in the genius era—is entirely out of place here; it must be replaced by an actor-network theory, also considering the forces of media technology, economy, etc.

Kleist seems to have anticipated all this: Creativity is not an independent cognitive competence preceding all action, merely 'translating' itself into practical activities or media. Creativity is experience, it is knowledge to be generated out of practices in the first place—knowledge that is dependent on the medium and material of its expression, on social interaction and mainly on the occupational domain in which one becomes creative. Defining abstract key qualifications such as flexibility or fluency is of little help here. The same holds true in my opinion for the defining of personal moods. I am thinking of Csikszentmihalyi's concept of 'flow'.

Proposition 3, therefore, is this: If creativity is not viewed from the perspective of the creative individual, but as experience and process, 'workplace studies' become necessary in order to allow for any 'theories of practice'.

Presumably, cooperative processes of creation in film function differently from those in industrial laboratories, management or sports. In the interest of an analysis of differing logics of creativity, 'workplace studies' become necessary, they become 'theories of practice'. They are particularly important today, since the relevance of the aesthetic discourse as a referential discourse for the theories of creativity has decreased considerably, due to the transfer of innovative power from the arts to digital information and biotechnologies. It would not be far-fetched to speak of a 'takeover' in reference to the designation of creative domains today. Since the Renaissance, the arts have been competing with technological progress and characterizing their innovations as genius or creative. Currently, the competition seems lost. A good example of this is Patrick Süskind's novel Perfume, in which the protagonist, Jean-Baptiste Grenouille, who is odourless and without distinctive expression, intends to become an original genius by murdering twenty-five virgins, sniffing their individual odours and combining them within himself. The audience, marvelling at this stylistic mixture of an assembled uniqueness, finally devours him out of sheer admiration. Süskind's historically rich novel personifies the sampling culture and the appropriation art of postmodernism and post-postmodernism, while, at the same time, it is a farewell to the progressive force of culture.

Proposition, 4, the last: The differentiation of specific concepts of creativity according to workplace, medium or material as the framework of creative action must be supplemented by an integrative creatology. The analysis of creativity must be understood as a trans-disciplinary and cross-cultural problem.

The question of creativity is marginalized in all disciplines today and there is—at least from my narrow German view—no comparison with epistemological interests, theories and results among the disciplines concerned with the analysis of creativity; no systematic cooperation of art and media studies, psychology, philosophy, sociology, pedagogy, cognitive science, evolutionary biology, chaos theory, ethnology, the research on artificial intelligence, etc. By means of such a cooperation, a literary scholar, for instance, concerned with surrealist aesthetics and working on concepts such as *écriture automatique* or *objet trouvé*, would have the opportunity to speak with a chaos theorist, who would have an entirely different grasp on contingency, taking it to be a measure of a subject's ignorance regarding the complexity of its surrounding system. And why shouldn't concepts such as 'preformation' or 'epigenesis'— prominent in evolutionary biology—become productive in the study of aesthetics? The same goes for cross-cultural comparison: Is there any concept similar to the Western notion of creatio ex nihilo (even though it is prominent only in monotheist cultures)? Any notion similar to the concept of the alliance of breath and mind in inspiration, e.g., in the Sanskrit *prana* or in the Chinese *chi*? Any notion similar to the Western alliance of creativity and melancholy? And could it be that the notions of creativity (or its equivalents) have changed with globalization?

Notes

1. Günter Blamberger, *Das Geheimnis des Schöpferischen oder, Ingenium est ineffabile? Studien zur Literaturgeschichte der Kreativität zwischen Goethezeit und Moderne* (Stuttgart: Metzler, 1991).

2. Rainer Maria Rilke, *Briefe*. Hg. v. Kurt Altheim in Verbindung mit Ruth Sieber-Rilke im Auftrag des Rilke-Archivs in Weimar (Frankfurt/M.: Insel-Verlag, 1980), S. 177ff.

3. 'Paul Cézanne, *Le baiser de la muse*, after Frillié, 1859–1860. Oil on canvas, 82.5 cm x 66 cm. Musée Granet,

Aix-en-Provence, France.' Sourced from Bildagentur für Kunst, Kultur und Geschichte Märkisches Ufer 16–18 DE – 10179 Berlin.

4. Cf. Friedrich Nietzsche, *Menschliches, Allzumenschliches. Ein Buch für freie Geister*. In: *Sämtliche Werke*. Kritische Studienausgabe in 15 Bdn. hg. v. Giorgio Colli u. Mazzino Montinari. München, Berlin, New York: dtv, 1980, Bd. 2, 146f. (quotations translated from German: 'Alle Grossen waren grosse Arbeiter' / 'Glauben an Inspiration', 'allzumenschliche' Illusion.

5. Copper Engraving 1514. This image is in the public domain because its copyright has expired.

6. Aristotle, *Problems*, trans. E.S. Forster. ed. Jonathan Barnes, vol. 2 (Princeton: Princeton University Press, 1984), 953a10ff. and 954b2f.

7. Mihaly Csikszentmihalyi, *Creativity: Flow and the Psychology of Discovery and Invention* (New York: Harper Collins, 1996).

8. Immanuel Kant, *Kant's Critique of Judgement*, trans. (with Introduction and Notes) J.H. Bernard (New York: Hafner Publishing, 1951), section 47.

9. Immanuel Kant, *Kant's Critique of Judgement*, trans. (with Introduction and Notes) J.H. Bernard (New York: Hafner Publishing, 1951), section 47.

10. Cf. Anthony Ashley-Cooper, 3rd Earl of Shaftesbury, *Soliloquy, or Advice to an Author*. In *Characteristicks of Men, Manners, Opinions, Times* (1711). Hg. von Bernhard Fabian u.a. Hildesheim (New York: Georg Olms Verlag, 1978), I, 207.

11. In German: 'Hier sitz' ich, forme Menschen/Nach meinem Bilde,/Ein Geschlecht, das mir gleich sei.' Cf. Johann Wolfgang von Goethe, *Sämtliche Werke, Briefe, Tagebücher und Gespräche.* Bd. 1: *Gedichte 1756–1799.* Hg. von Karl Eibl. (Frankfurt/M.: Deutscher Klassiker-Verlag, 1987), S. 329f. For the English translation cf. David Wellbery, *The Specular Moment. Goethe's Early Lyric and the Beginnings of Romanticism* (Stanford: Stanford UP, 1996), 288–90.

12. For all quotations from this essay cf. Heinrich von Kleist, *Selected Writings,* ed. and trans. David Constantine (London: J.M. Dent, 1997), 405–09.

Chinese Creativity: Past, Present and Future

Weihua Niu

It is the human being who is able to extend the *dao*, not the *dao* that is able to extend the human being.
—Confucius, *The Analects* (Cai 2006, 90)

In the past few decades, the world has witnessed China's rapid growth not only in its economy, with a sustained annual growth rate averaging over 10 per cent since the 1980s, but also in other areas such as science, technology, literature, art and education. The words 'innovation' and 'creativity' are now commonly used by Chinese leaders, policymakers, school administrators, entrepreneurs, scientists, artists, scholars as well as ordinary Chinese, reflecting a keen interest and dire need for creative development within the whole society.

63

From the perspective of the state, innovation and creativity are conceived as the soul of the nation's progress and, together, they make up the inexhaustible motivational force driving the prosperity of its country and the source of the eternal vitality of a political party (Jiang 2000, 55–56). Starting in the mid-1990s, reform and development in China have focused increasingly on promoting innovation and creativity, even including them in national strategic planning during the last few years (Peng and Plucker 2012).

From the public perspective, creativity is considered an important currency for success. Books such as *Enhancing Creativity of Gifted Children* (Khatena 2000; Kai, Wang and Xu 2003) and *Whole Brain Super Creative* (Wang 2005) are bestsellers and are prominently displayed in bookstores in China. Educational programmes aimed at promoting creativity in children in the fields of art, science and technology, too, have become increasingly popular in some major Chinese cities. The successful running of several newly developed reality and talent TV programmes such as *Sing My Songs*,[1] *The Brain*[2] and

---

[1] A Chinese reality talent show similar to the *Voice of China*; however, a major difference is that contestants of *Sing My Songs* must perform their original composition, not cover songs by other artists.

[2] A scientific reality, talent and game show originating in Germany but produced in China. The show's aim is to find people whose brainpower is beyond that of ordinary people.

Swordsman Comics[3] are examples of the craving for not only pure entertainment but also indigenous forms of creativity.

Such fanaticism for creativity in twenty-first-century China reflects implicit belief among ordinary Chinese people that

(1) creativity is an important quality for individual and national success in global competition;
(2) the Chinese are lagging behind in creativity and innovation compared to others; and
(3) like any other trait, creativity can be enhanced through proper training and education. In fact, it is not only the Chinese who are worried about their inferiority in the realm of creativity and are eager to catch up with the rest of the world. People with similar cultural backgrounds—such as those from East Asia—share the same concerns and zeal (Niu 2006; Peng and Plucker 2012).

In 2001, Aik Kwang Ng's book *Why Asians Are Less Creative than Westerners* made it quickly to the bestseller list in the author's home country, Singapore, and has been widely

---

[3] A Chinese reality talent show started in Spring 2014, aiming to find talent in the realm of comedy. The name of the show is the same as a very famous martial arts book and movie, although the show itself does not intend to find talents in martial arts.

circulated in both academic and public fields worldwide. This book perpetuates a long-held assumption that the so-called Confucian-heritage Asian societies are less creative than their counterparts in societies such as North America and Europe, where liberal individualism prevails. Ng postulates that the growth and development of creativity in Eastern societies such as China, Japan, Korea, Singapore, Taiwan and Hong Kong is inhibited by these factors: Eastern values concerning the hierarchy of society; a greater emphasis on social order and harmony between family and society; concern with face (*mian-zi*, 面子); a desire to gain the social approval of the group; and a negative view of societal conflict. Nevertheless, towards the end of the book, Ng concludes that although Asians may be less creative than Westerners, they can gain freedom and become more creative when a suitable environment (albeit a more Westernized environment) is put in place and proper training is provided. He then provides ten guidelines to help Asians be more creative and to achieve collectively a more creative Asian society (Ng 2000).

The above stereotype echoes a common belief shared by some early theorists in social sciences and humanities in the early-twentieth century. The thesis states that Confucianism places greater emphasis on conformation and maintaining harmony with others rather than on individualization or becoming independent and being critical; adjusting oneself to the world rather than changing it. They are, therefore, inimical to the development of individual creativity, even to the extent of blocking the economic growth of society. For example, comparing and contrasting the social and economic development of Chinese and Western societies, Max Weber (1864–1920), a founding figure of sociology, argued that, deeply influenced by the Confucian and the Taoist world view, the Chinese people, compared to those from the West, lack the spirit of capitalism. John King Fairbank, a leading American sinologist, along with his colleagues, claimed that within China, at least from the nineteenth century, 'minor growth, innovation and technological change may occur but . . . not sufficient to break the rigid and inhibiting bonds of the traditional framework of social and economic institutions' (Eckstein, Fairbank and Yang 1960), suggesting that Chinese culture is not conducive to individual creativity. Amazed by the extraordinary achievements in science and the rich civilization of the ancient Chinese, but still lagging behind the West in science and technology, especially since the nineteenth century, Joseph Needham, a renowned British sinologist posited his famous question: 'Why did the Industrial Revolution not originate in China?' (Needham 1956). More recently, Howard Gardner, a contemporary psychologist and educationalist from Harvard University, asserted that the Chinese educational system may have a stifling effect on the development of creativity (Gardner 1989). He also posited that the creativity exhibited in the West is more revolutionary, while China fosters the other type of creativity, namely, evolutionary creativity (Gardner 1993, 1996).

Scholars most recently challenged this thesis through an examination of the industrial rise of East Asia (Japan, South Korea, Singapore, Taiwan, Hong Kong and, most recently, Mainland China) and its relationship to Confucianism. As a shared core-cultural heritage, Confucianism and Confucian ethics are concerned with one's relationship with others, and maintaining harmony within a community. They emphasize hard work, thrift and self-reliance, all of which are believed to be conducive rather than inhibiting to the economic development of these societies in today's world. According to Tu Weiming, a contemporary American sinologist, one important reason is that the current economic culture is much more human-oriented than in the early stage of industrialization; therefore, community-oriented capitalism is more competitive than individual-oriented classical capitalism. That may be the most important legacy of Confucianism to modern times (Tu 1989).

This new interpretation of the impact of Confucianism on societal economic growth can also apply to creativity. Perhaps, Chinese culture does not necessarily inhibit the development of creativity; instead, some forms of creativity indigenous to Chinese culture may not be fully appreciated by theorists. If Confucius-heritage societies, such as China, do not necessarily hinder creativity, what exactly has creativity meant to the Chinese, both in the past and the present? Do the Chinese view creativity differently from Westerners?

Philosophical roots of Chinese creativity

Before engaging in an examination of ancient Chinese philosophical roots of creativity, one needs to be aware that the words used by the ancient Chinese to describe creativity (*chuang zao li*, 创造力 or *chuang zao xing*, 创造性[4]) are different from those used by contemporary Chinese. Most sinologists have agreed that the closest word for 'creativity' in ancient Chinese is *dao* (way, 道). Other similar terms include *tian* (heaven, 天), *tai-yi* (the Great One, 太一), *taiji* (the Great Ultimate, 太极), *yin–yang* (阴阳) and *cheng* (integrity, 诚) (Ames and Hall 2001; Berthrong 1998; Niu and Sternberg 2006; Wen 2009).

Etymologically, the Chinese character of dao (道) is composed of two elements: *shou* (head, 首), suggesting

---

[4] Two Chinese spelling systems are used in discussing Chinese documents. One is *pinyin*, which is used primarily in Mainland China, and the other system is *Wade-Giles*, which is primarily used in Taiwan and overseas. This essay uses the system of *pinyin*, accompanied by the Chinese characters in simplified form.

to lead, and *ya* (foot or walking, 辵, 辶 or 走), which literally means 'leading from the beginning'. Generally speaking, dao has two broad meanings: 'the origin of everything' and 'the paths that people later walked on'. In other words, the word dao implies both the origin and the continued production of new things. No doubt, the word dao and other similar words, such as tai-yi and taiji, are important concepts in ancient Chinese philosophy, especially in Confucianism and Taoism (Schwartz 1985).

In our 2006 paper, Sternberg and I (Niu and Sternberg 2006) compared the Biblical view of 'God's creation from nothing' (ex nihilo, we called it divine-inspired creativity) and the Chinese cosmological interpretation of the creation process (dao, taiji and yin–yang changes, we called them natural creativity). We concluded that the concept of creativity in both the West and the East emanated from a mystical tradition, either theistic or cosmic. In other words, creativity was universally believed to have come from a source outside human beings. Humans do not create but simply imitate God's creation (according to the Western Biblical idea) or connect themselves to the heavens, dao, through meditation (according to the Eastern Taoist idea). Since both cultures attribute creativity to a higher source, the concepts of creativity, for both ancient Westerners and Chinese, possessed the defining feature of goodness, including moral goodness. In the Chinese mind, such goodness included goodness towards a collective being or contribution to the whole society. The difference between the two traditions is the emphasis on the feature of novelty in creativity. In the West, novelty is a defining feature of creativity in the Biblical view of God's creation; in the Chinese tradition, it is emphasized. For the Chinese, there is no clear beginning of the universe, tao, nor a creator for it. The nature of dao is its everlasting changes, which may or may not bring new forms of everything.

I have since then revised the thesis regarding the distinction between the Western and the Chinese philosophical roots of creativity. A full explanation of the Confucian views of creativity was included in a special issue on American and Chinese creativity in the *Journal of Creative Behavior* (Niu 2012). Here, I would like to highlight again some of the major themes illustrated in both papers.

Contrast of *creatio in situ* and *creatio ex nihilo*

The first theme of my recent paper (Niu 2012) is that the concept of creativity comes from different philosophical roots in the West and China and, therefore, has different meanings (Niu 2012). The English word 'creativity' comes from a Biblical idea of God and God's creation, creatio ex nihilo (creation out of nothing). This concept is missing in Chinese wisdom. A parallel concept, creatio in situ, creation in context, should be viewed as the alternative to creatio ex nihilo, when describing the Chinese notion of creativity.

Many sinologists have examined the concept of creatio ex nihilo by reviewing some ancient Chinese documents, including the *Book of Changes* (*Yijing*), its commentaries, and *The Great One Gives Birth to the Waters* (*Taiyishengshui*, 太一生水) (Allan 2003; Fingarette 1983; Wen 2009). *Taiyishengshui* was written on fourteen bamboo strips, and is part of the collection called the *Guodian Chu Slips* (*Guodian Chujian*, 郭店楚簡), which was unearthed in 1993 in one of the Guodian tombs in Hubei Province. The tombs are believed to date back to the fourth century BC, and the texts on the bamboo slips would have been written before or close to the time of burial. *Taiyishengshui* is believed to be the earliest record of Chinese cosmogony available. The opening paragraph of *Taiyishengshui* is:

> The Great One gave birth to water; water returned and assisted The Great One, in this way developing heaven. Heaven returned and assisted The Great One, in this way developing the earth. Heaven and the earth repeatedly assisted each other, in this way developing the gods above and below. The gods above and below repeatedly assisted each other, in this way developing Yin and Yang. Yin and Yang repeatedly assisted each other, in this way developing

the four seasons. The four seasons repeatedly assisted each other, in this way assisting moist and dry. Moist and dry repeatedly assisted each other, in this way developing the circle of the year, and the process came to an end (Allan 2003, 261).

(太一生水， 水反輔大一，是以成天。天反輔大一，是以成地。天地[复相輔]也，是以成神明。神明复[相]輔也，是以成陰陽。陰陽复相輔也，是以成四時。四時复相輔也，是以成滄熱。滄熱复相輔也，是以成濕燥。濕燥复相輔也，成歲而止。)

The idea of creatio in situ is clearly reflected in this passage with the keyword 'assist' or 'help' (fu, 輔), suggesting that not only is the creative process attributable to the creator, but also to the continued collaboration between the creator and the creature, which means 'co-creativity'. For example, while The Great One gave birth to water, the same water—the creature—came back and collaterally assisted The Great One in giving birth to heaven. In the same way, heaven came back and collaterally assisted The Great One in giving birth to the earth. It is clear that the creation process of The Great One is different from the Biblical idea of 'God's creation'. In the Biblical tradition, God is a personalized, independent agency outside the world which He created, the world which He created from nothing (creatio ex nihilo).

According to Roger T. Ames from the University of Hawaii, there are at least five fundamental differences between the two concepts of creativity, creatio ex nihilo and creatio in situ (Ames 2005).

First, in creatio ex nihilo, God, the divine creator, is an independent agency, separating Himself from the world, His creatures. However, in creatio in situ, creation exists in a pre-existing context so that the creator and the creature are mutually implicated and continuous.

Second, whereas ex nihilo focuses on originality, in situ emphasizes the enhanced significance due to the ongoing productivity of its applications in the continuing present. In other words, to the ancient Chinese, creativity is meaningless unless the creator interacts with the context and they continue to produce new things together.

Third, as a result of being brought forth into existence from nothing, the creature in creatio ex nihilo is totally dependent upon the creator. In contrast, in creatio in situ, the creator and the creature are interdependent: the dynamic relationship between the creator and the context is the source of continuing creativity.

Fourth, while the creatio ex nihilo model needs to appeal only to the creator as the source of novelty, the creatio in situ model needs to appeal to the whole process, including the past history, the development and the future. In other words, creatio in situ emphasizes the importance of both the precedents and the consequences of the creative action.

Lastly, in the ex nihilo model, there was a nihil or void before creation, whereas in the in situ model, there is no notion of a void, and creativity is the spontaneous emergence of novelty in a continuing present. In other words, change is constant; creativity happens when novelty is produced in accordance with the change of the context.

Simply put, while creativity resides in the power of the creator according to the Biblical view, it is the very nature of everlasting interaction between the creator and the context that results in creativity according to Chinese wisdom. Some scholars called such a notion 'co-creativity' (Ames 2005), or 'contextual creativity' (Wen 2009).

The Confucian view of creativity

The concept of co-creativity (creatio in situ) or contextual creativity was extended and explained much more elaborately by Confucian scholars, even though the concept may appear to have come from a Taoist tradition. Here are some important features of a Confucian view of creativity:

Human focus

Unlike the Biblical notion of creativity, from the very beginning, Confucianism has been concerned with its notion of creativity, with humans and with acknowledged human creativity. The quote used at the very beginning of this essay suggests that Confucius believed that human beings have the ability and the disposition to establish the world and grow it. Human beings have created civilization and many other new things to make the world advance through *creatio in situ*. However, they are not the masters of the world. The world in which they live is not a world created out of nothing; rather, they have created it based on the changes of the context and the experiences they have had while interacting with the context. Human beings strive to comprehend the world to the extent of their ability, but will never reach a final understanding of the world. Therefore, it is the interaction between them and the environment that has brought forth new things, and this will continue to result in the creation of more new things.

The notion that human beings are responsible for the progress of the world is inherent in Chinese culture, and this can be seen from some famous Chinese idioms such as 'Man's will, not Heaven, decides' (人定胜天); 'Man proposes, Heaven disposes' (谋事在人，成事在天); and 'The time isn't as important as the terrain, but the terrain isn't as important as unity with the people' (天时不如地利，地

利不如人和). Some of these idioms, such as 'Man's will, not Heaven, decides', have been taken to extreme forms in industrialized China, and have become an issue when people over-exploit nature in pursuit of economic prosperity.

Co-creativity or contextual creativity

Related to the first feature, the Confucian view of creativity concerns the relationship between the creator and the context. Being sensitive and responsive to one's situation and working productively with the environment is the key to human creativity. This does not mean mere passivity; on the contrary, people need to be flexible and open-minded and actively shape the environment, but, at the same time, to allow the environment to shape itself. Wen (2009) used the term 'contextual creativity' to explain further the Confucian notion of creativity:

> The meaning of contextual creativity thus starts from the reflexivity of purpose as a correlative relationship between people and their environments. From this co-creative world view, the world comes to us as an actualization of contextual purposes and intentions, and we foster the growth of meaning from an under-determinate state to a determinate one. Therefore, the contextual creativity of people in the world is the process of commanding meaning and facilitating the emergence of significance. (p. 89)

Originality and appropriateness

According to the modern definition of creativity, the defining features of creativity are originality and appropriateness (Amabile 1996; Csikszentmihalyi 1996; Sternberg and Lubart 1995, 1999).

In Confucian doctrines, the notion of originality is not directly addressed but implied through the belief that creativity occurs in everlasting production through human interaction with the context. Since the production and the context are always changing and are somewhat different from the past, they are new. This newness, however, is a relative term and it is always situated between the past and the future. Confucius himself highly appreciated tradition, and proposed a model to his followers about how an ideal scholar could be produced through learning from tradition. The word 'new' or 'novel' in Confucianism is never a sharp breakaway from tradition; rather, it can be seen as an extension of tradition. For example, Confucius said in *The Analects*, chapter 2.11, 'If one is able to acquire new knowledge by reviewing old knowledge, he is qualified to be a teacher' (温故而知新，可以为师矣) (Cai 2006, 19).

Therefore, it is reasonable to believe that, in Confucianism, originality is still an important feature of creativity, but emphasis is being laid on a gradual and continuing change from the past. In a way, it follows the concept of evolution rather than revolution.

On the other hand, in Confucianism, appropriateness plays a vital role in judging creativity. The word appropriateness (yi, 义) means doing what is fitting. According to Gramham (1989), yi is one's sense of appropriateness which enables one to act in a proper and fitting manner, given a specific situation. The focus of yi is on the environment. Thus, signification comes from a proper creative response to situational changes, which means that intentions are properly timed and responsive to emerging circumstances.

An important concept in Confucianism is the notion of zhongyong (doctrine of the mean, 中庸), which was misinterpreted as taking the middle stand and not going to the extreme, and hence, being conservative and less adventurous. However, the word is actually made of two characters: zhong (appropriateness, 中) and yong (to apply, 庸). Its actual meaning is to know when to do what, and to act according to the situation. A Chinese psychologist, Yang, explained zhongyong as a metacognitive thinking style, in which an individual observes the changes in the outside world and actively modifies his or her own thinking. She said, 'Zhong does not necessarily mean "the middle way", it actually means to find an appropriate point between the two extremes when taking into account the nature of the two extremes' (Yang 2009).

Creative process and creative education

The Confucian notion of creativity places great emphasis on a person's purposeful engagement in the creative process. A person has to study purposefully and build up his or her own character through self-cultivation (*xiushen*, 修身), engage in and understand the environment through investigation (*gewu*, 格物), and become comprehensive in their understanding of things (*zhizhi*, 致知). Only through this procedure can creativity be achieved. In other words, in order to work in collaboration with the environmental context, creative individuals must first establish themselves in their local environment. They are always situated in appropriate positions so that they can maximize their influence within the world. The way to achieve this is through self-cultivation. Confucian self-cultivation is a process in which a person progresses from studying (*xue*, 学) to actual awareness (*jue*, 觉) or greatness. The way to achieve greatness through learning lies in demonstrating real character, in cherishing the common people and in making a commitment to doing what is best. Such a course of learning can only be set after one has made this commitment. Only by setting such a course can one find equilibrium, only by finding equilibrium can one be deliberate in what one does, and only by being deliberate in what one does can one get what one is after. There is the important and the incidental in things, and a beginning and an end to what we do. It is by realizing what should be given priority that one gets closer to the proper way.

In short, the Confucian notion of creativity focuses on an individual's autonomy and on his proper engagement with the context. The following characteristics are included:

(1) Human beings have the potential to create and to play an important role in the creation of the world and human civilization.
(2) Human beings are not the sole creators of the world; they have to work in collaboration with the context surrounding the world, and act appropriately in order to achieve creativity, hence the notion of co-creativity or contextual creativity.
(3) Originality is a defining feature for creativity, but it is seen as a continuation from the past, the present and the future, not a breakaway.
(4) Appropriateness—fitting to the changing context—describes how humans and context work in collaboration in the creative process, hence its high value in creativity.
(5) Human creativity is a purposeful activity and, in order to achieve creativity, a person has to continue to learn from others, control his own emotions and

behaviour to build up a character that is suitable to the environment (self-cultivation).

(6) The individual has to be open-minded and actively engaged in investigating the environment, and has to allow the environment to change him or her, and to eventually reach a comprehensive understanding and full awareness of things in the world.

The Taoist view of creativity

Even though Confucianism has long been a major school of thought in China and was given a dominant position by the ruling class starting from the second century, it is necessary to know that there are many other important philosophical traditions and religions, including Taoism, legalism, Buddhism, naturalism and other schools of thoughts, which have shaped the thoughts and values of the Chinese. Among them, Taoism is believed to have had the strongest impact on the Chinese notion of creativity (Chang 1970). In our 2006 paper, Sternberg and I discussed the Taoist view of creativity and its impact on the Chinese people's creative activity, particularly in the domains of literature and arts. Contrary to Confucianism— where purposeful engagement and active acquirement of knowledge are important for achieving creativity—Taoist scholars believe that the creative process is the process of the inner attainment of dao, when all the distinctions between subject (self) and object (non-self) vanish. In order to achieve higher levels of creativity, individuals have to lose themselves through meditation, in many ways similar to the state of flow, which is described by a modern psychologist, Csikszcntmihalyi (1988, 1997) as an important stage to engage in creative activities.

In his book, *Creativity and Taoism: A Study of Chinese Philosophy, Art and Poetry,* Chang (1970) explained that the Taoist idea of high creative achievement could be manipulated through the 'invisible ground of sympathy', in which people set themselves free of all old knowledge they previously held, and enter a state where everything breaks through its own shell and fuses with every other thing. That is the highest stage of creativity people can achieve. Once a person has this great sympathy, he or she can be absolutely free to connect with the universe, and everything he does is highly creative. The Taoist idea of returning and losing oneself has had a great impact on the Chinese literati and their creative activity throughout Chinese history, especially in the domains of poetry and painting. The great Chinese poets and artists who, through meditation and self-cultivation, penetrated to this great sympathy produced a large amount of truly great work. They are thought to owe a great debt to ancient Taoist theory and its methods.

The above discussion on the ancient philosophical roots of Chinese creativity illustrates two totally different approaches to how the Chinese view the creative process: one, through purposeful engagement in and active acquisition of knowledge, and the other, through quietude and meditation in order to reach the stage of 'losing oneself' to achieve connection to the universe. Both notions of creativity have greatly impacted the Chinese and continue to influence the way contemporary Chinese perceive creativity.

Conceptions of creativity of contemporary Chinese

In psychology, interest in studying the contemporary Chinese concept of creativity started less than twenty years ago (for a review Niu and Sternberg 2002; Rudowicz 2003, 2004). There are two main approaches to studying people's concept of creativity. One is through examining explicit theories developed by social scientists based on empirical-based studies and systematic observation, and the other is through studying lay people's beliefs or prototypes of the concept, which is generally referred to as the implicit theories (Sternberg 1985; Runco 1990).

Explicit theories of creativity in the Chinese context

Many theories have been developed over the past half-century, explaining the nature of creativity and the mechanisms that facilitate the development of creativity. Most predominately, these theories originated in North America. The most popular ones include the psychometric approach (Guilford 1956; Torrance 1966, 1988), the componential theory (Amabile 1983, 1996), the systems view (Csikszentmihalyi 1988, 1996), the historiometry approach (Simonton 1991, 1996, 2000), the three-faced model (Sternberg, 1988) and the investment theory (Sternberg and Lubert 1991, 1995, 1999). Some of these explicit theories have shaped the way creativity was perceived in the field of psychology and have been accepted by the public. For example, the idea of divergent thinking and its measurement, such as the Torrance Tests of Creative Thinking (TTCT), has been widely accepted by both the public and psychology practitioners as the authentic way of defining and measuring creativity.

Many of these theories and measurements were introduced to the rest of the world as well as Chinese societies. These theories were used to explain Chinese creativity, and measures derived from North America, such as TTCT and other similar divergent thinking measures, were widely used by Chinese psychologists to study the creativity of the Chinese and to compare the creativity of the Chinese and Westerners. Only recently have scholars started to search for the cultural roots of Chinese creativity and to come up with theories to explain the meaning of creativity in the Chinese context.

Creativity and Taoism

As mentioned in the preceding section, Chang (1970) gives a detailed discussion on the Taoist view of creativity.

After Chang, Kuo (1996) elaborated further on the Taoist view and drew a parallel between Taoist principles and practice and Western theories of creativity, and called it the Taoist Psychology of Creativity. For example, the Taoist concept of losing or liquidating the learnt knowledge can be interpreted as an abandonment of tunnel vision or a freedom from the restrictions of past experience so that individuals can be more open and receptive to new experience. Another parallel between Taoism and Western theories of creativity is found in regard to the interconnection of the human mind with the dao of the universe. Therefore, the Taoist approach to achieving creativity is to search inside, rather than reaching outside. The notion that Tao exists inside oneself implies that intuitive knowledge, dao, comes from incubation or insight, not from the writings of other people. Only the knowledge intuited by oneself is true knowledge or personal knowledge, which can be called Tao or great wisdom. Tao's attitude of let-be, non-interference and not-labelling, naming or classifying can also be interpreted as free will, or allocentrically oriented, which is often found to be associated with characteristics of creative artists. In this article, Kuo also talks about Taoist sanity and points out some health benefits of Taoist creativity. According to him, the emphasis on tranquillity in the process of Taoist creativity makes artists much saner than their Western counterparts. This can be attributed to the nature of Chinese art as a symbolic expression of the individual Taoist's experiences, while Western art tends to function as an outlet for subconscious sexual and destructive fantasies.

Confucianism and creativity

Several scholars have examined the relationship between Confucianism and creativity. Some came from searching a philosophical tradition for the meaning of creativity in Chinese classics, similar to the fashion in the preceding section of this article (Ames 2005; Niu 2012; Wen 2009). Others adopted an empirical approach in examining the relationship between Confucianism and creativity through measurements and scales designed to measure these concepts among ordinary people. For example, Kim and her colleagues did a series of studies to examine Confucianism and creativity using Korean samples. In these studies, she used the Eastern–Western Perspective Scale (EWPS) to measure the degree to which an individual held Confucian ideals, and the TTCT-Figural to measure creativity (Kim 2005, 2007; Kim, Lee, Chae, Andersen and Lawrence 2011). In one study, they examined how the integration of Confucianism affects Korean educators' creativity (Kim et al. 2011). The results showed a negative correlation between the scores on the two measurements: EWPS and TTCT. She also found a gender difference in the endorsement of the Confucian ideals. She concluded that Korean male educators hold more Confucian ideals than female educators, which may be explained by the male-dominated aspects of Confucianism. The results also support that some characteristics of Confucianism, such as unconditional obedience, gender inequality, gender role expectations and suppression of expression, may present a cultural block to the development of creativity.

Horizontal vs vertical domain in painting

Li (1997) proposed a theory regarding the relationship between domain and creativity, in which two types of domains were discussed: horizontal vs vertical. Horizontal domains allow novelty to occur in all dimensions, resulting in divergent developments of the domain, whereas vertical domains possess certain stable elements that are existentially fundamental to the domain, thus permitting alternation only around certain dimensions. Two apparently similar painting domains—modern Western painting (as an example of horizontal domain) and Chinese traditional ink painting (as an example of vertical domain)—were carefully examined, along five structural parameters: the aim, the methods, the symbol systems and their multifaceted natures, allowing creativity to occur in an indefinite number of dimensions. It was concluded that the domains showed different levels of constraints to creativity. Horizontal domains allow creativity to occur in an indefinite number of dimensions, resulting in creativity which deviates significantly from the previously established practice, leading it in multiple—essentially unpredictable—directions, whereby they are more revolutionary. In contrast, vertical domains allow creativity to be expressed only in one dimension, resulting in creativity that is not far from the conventional core, whereby they are more evolutionary. Although the focus was only on painting, the thesis examined the way Chinese creativity is defined and appreciated.

Creative personality in Chinese poetry

Using a thematic analysis approach, Sundararaja (2004) examined the personality of ancient Chinese artists using as source an ancient Chinese poetry critique book, called *The Twenty-Four Categories of Poetry* (二十四诗品), written by Sikong Tu (司空图, 837–908), a famous poet of the late Tang Dynasty (618–907 AD). Sundararaja found that the prototype of the ideal Chinese poet was one who was arrogant but not hostile (non-aggressive, non-assertive, non-argumentative). The Chinese prototype of creativity has some similarity to those found in Western literature, which includes autonomy, nonconformity, openness to experience and a high intrinsic motivation to engage in creative production. However, there are some unique characteristics in the context of Chinese aesthetics. One is a concern for the wholeness of beauty which is using extensively complementary dialectics as an attempt to reveal the larger whole. Another unique characteristic is the importance of self-reflexivity and self-cultivation of Chinese artists. Finally, Chinese artists who are interested in self-improvement are less likely to harbour symptoms of psychopathology than those who do not include self-transformation in the agenda of their creative endeavours. It confirms Kuo's (1996) theory of Taoist sanity and Chinese creativity.

In summary, explicit theories of Chinese creativity firmly embrace the traditional view of creativity, in which

(1) the creative process is viewed as a process of searching for a connection between oneself and the universe through meditation or self-cultivation; and

(2) the Chinese notion of creativity shows more concern for appropriateness and less concern for novelty, shows flexibility and open-mindedness, lays a greater emphasis on evolution than on revolution and also has high ethical and moral standards.

Implicit theories of creativity of contemporary Chinese

A useful approach to examining whether the explicit theories of Chinese creativity are consistent with the general beliefs of contemporary Chinese is by studying the implicit theories of creativity. This method was initiated by scholars from the West and then extended to other cultures (Csikszentmihalyi 1996, 1999; Helsen 1996; Montgomery, Bull and Balche 1993; Runco, Johnson and Bear 1993; Runco and Bahleda 1987; Sternberg 1985). The general approach is to ask lay people about their perceptions of the characteristics of creative individuals. Results from studying implicit theories of Westerners suggest that creative individuals are described as intelligent, open-minded, logical, capable, imaginative, energetic, active, motivated, willing to take a stand, inquisitive, curious, adventurous, ambitious, self-confident, determined, enthusiastic, free-spirited, nonconformist, individualistic, confident, assertive, daring, artistic, with good aesthetic taste and with a sense of humour.

Results from studying implicit theories of Chinese people are in a large part consistent with those of the West, in which certain characteristics such as novelty, independence, imagination, innovation, power, energy, self-confidence, flexibility, intelligence, willingness to try and breaking away from tradition are found to be closely associated with creativity. There are also some unique characteristics of the Chinese perception of creativity. For example, Rudowicz and Hui (1997) find that characteristics relating to having a sense of humour and an appreciation for aesthetics and art consistently—which are reported in North American implicit theories—are absent in concepts of creativity of the general public of Hong Kong. Artistic taste and humour are also almost non-existent in the implicit concepts of undergraduates in Mainland China, Hong Kong and Taiwan (Rudowicz and Yue 2000), and of Hong Kong teachers (Chan and Chan 1999). Some unique characteristics were reported by Chinese participants in describing creativity, which were missing in the American samples. Those characteristics include 'making a contribution to the progress of society', 'being an inspiration to other people' and 'being appreciated by others'. Interestingly, differing from the explicit theories regarding the Chinese conception of creativity, ethical standards, such as a sense of responsibility, honesty, self-discipline and selflessness, were not reported as being associated with creative individuals in the conception of creativity of Chinese students from Hong Kong and Mainland China (Rudowicz and Hui 1997, 1998; Rudowicz and Yue 2000; Rudowicz 2003).

Clearly, there is a great deal of overlap between the Chinese and the Western notion of creativity in implicit theories. Contemporary Chinese seem to have adopted a more Westernized conception of creativity, which somewhat deviates from the cultural traditions proposed by the explicit theorists. Some unique characteristics of creativity found in contemporary Chinese, such as an emphasis on contribution to society, being an inspiration to others and being appreciated by others, may suggest that the cultural influence on contemporary Chinese conception of creativity is still present, although in a less pervasive way, as proposed by the explicit theories.

What is Chinese creativity?

The above review indicates that Chinese culture has a long history of recognizing and celebrating human creativity. Coming as they did from different cultural traditions, the ancient Chinese held different views from their Western counterparts regarding what constitutes creativity. The fundamental differences between the two traditions are the focus of creativity; the emphasis on the dual nature of creativity, novelty and appropriateness; and the role which humans play in creativity. In the West, the focus of creativity has historically been on the creator, whereas, in the Chinese context, the emphasis lies on the interaction between the creator and the context. Although originality is an important feature of creativity in Chinese culture—influenced predominately by Confucianism—the Chinese notion of creativity has paid much more attention to the appropriateness of both creative individuals and their products. Also affected by other philosophical traditions, creativity is viewed as making a connection between oneself and nature; therefore, a useful approach to creativity is by losing oneself or through meditation.

Additionally, while Western tradition holds that God is the creator and that human beings do not create but only imitate, the Chinese have historically believed that humans play an important role in the creation of the world and of human civilization. These differences in philosophical views on creativity are believed to have an impact on contemporary views of creativity in the two cultures. However, results of studying the implicit views of creativity of contemporary Chinese—especially among college students—indicate that contemporary Chinese seem to adopt a more Western notion of creativity rather than their own cultural tradition.

There is a division between the implicit and the explicit theories in perceiving creativity in the contemporary Chinese context. It should be noted that most explicit theories are derived from an examination of the Chinese philosophic roots and an observation of the creativity exhibited in traditional Chinese art domains. Research on explicit theories used the ancient Chinese vocabulary for Chinese creativity, such as dao, whereas research on implicit theories always used the vocabulary derived from a Western concept. It is not clear to what extent language contributes to the incongruence the implicit and the explicit theories of Chinese creativity. It should also be noted that most of the psychological research in studying Chinese creativity has used, as the main participants, college students—the section of the population most influenced by the West. Their views on creativity may not necessarily reflect how creativity is nurtured and valued in the Chinese context, especially in the domains where Chinese values predominate, such as in the arts. More studies are needed to scrutinize the question regarding culture, domain and individual creativity. Moreover, most measurements used to capture creativity are based on the Western notion of creativity, even when they are used to study the creativity of the Chinese. Therefore, it is important to revisit each side of research and to find an appropriate way of examining the nature of Chinese creativity.

Finally, I wish to highlight three major characteristics of Chinese creativity, which may help to broaden our understanding of this important question in the future. First, unlike their Western counterparts, it is natural for the Chinese people to believe that everyone has the potential to be creative. One does not need to be a genius or possess special abilities for that. Such a belief is also associated with the belief that creativity can be exhibited in any domain or area, including areas which are perhaps less prestigious and measureable, such as creativity in the culinary arts. It is hard not to be astonished by the sophistication and elegance expressed by ordinary Chinese people in their pursuit of culinary creativity. In fact, the creative usage of various ingredients and cooking methods has often been initiated by the limitation of natural resources. For example, people living in the north-west part of China, with many mountains and very few rivers, were restricted by the scarcity of edible plants. Housewives had to be creative to present their families with varieties of food. Working continuously with the environment, passing on their creativity and wisdom through generations to refine the art, the ordinary Chinese learned to appreciate how to make the most of their limited resources. Yutang Lin, a famous Chinese writer and inventor who spent most of his life outside China, once claimed that 'the Chinese might well be inferior to others in creating wealth; however, they greatly excelled others in making the most of their limited resources' (Lin 1935/2010). In many ways, working with the environment and making the best of it reflects the concept of contextual creativity, or creatio in situ discussed earlier. It proves that this indigenous type of creativity still exists in China and, in fact, is widely practised and appreciated among contemporary Chinese.

Everyone can be creative, in different ways, on different scales, and may also minimize the individual contribution in building up the Big-C, the rare and breakthrough kind of creativity that can lead to an eminent contribution to a field. To the Chinese, any creative production or renovation is seen as a part of continuing evolution, not a single individual event. Every innovation is seen as simply making a connection between history and the future.

Therefore, no single person should take the sole credit. That may be attributable to the difficulties in China to implement and protect intellectual property.

The second characteristic came from the Taoist tradition, in which the creative process is viewed as allowing people to set themselves free of all old knowledge, to enter a state where one can achieve sympathy or make a connection between the individual and the original stage of the universe. Such a process can be achieved through meditation, which is similar to the stage of mindfulness. More and more Western scholars have utilized mindfulness and meditation in programmes other than creative education. Clearly, given the fact that this approach has been practised in Chinese societies for many centuries to promote individual creativity, it has great potential for revival in today's world.

The third characteristic of Chinese creativity comes from the Confucian notion of purposeful engagement and self-cultivation. In other words, to be creative, a person must set up a goal and put a great deal of effort into learning and practising. There is a popular Chinese saying: 'Practice makes perfect' (*Shu Neng Sheng Qiao*, 熟能生巧). The Chinese character *Qiao*, 巧, has multiple meanings: 'skilful', 'craftsmanship', 'clever', 'adept', 'cunning', 'felicitous' and 'artful'. In fact, the best translation here would be 'artful' or 'craftsmanship', as the saying is often used to describe a person who achieves a certain level of art by constant practice. The literary translation of the saying is, 'Practice can produce craftsmanship'.

The idiom comes from the *Collection of Essays of Ouyang Xiu* (欧阳修, 1007–72), in which this story is recorded: Duke Chen is a master of archery and he likes to boast of his skills by practising in public. One day, an old oil peddler comes by and shows his indifference to the duke's skill. He is not impressed by Duke Chen's skills, and comments: 'Your abilities are just okay, nothing special. You've gained your accuracy through constant practice. That's all.' Deeply hurt, Duke Chen challenges the peddler to an archery competition. The old man says nothing, but puts a gourd bottle on the ground and covers its mouth with a copper coin. He then scoops out a ladle of oil from his big jar, holds it high and begins to fill the bottle. A thread of oil comes down from the ladle into the bottle just through a hole of the coin. Everybody looking on watches with amazement. But the old man says, 'This is nothing special. I can do this because I have practised it a lot.'

This story is very popular in present-day China due to the fact that it has been included in the middle-school textbooks for over three decades. The story and the saying, 'Shu Neng Sheng Qiao', are often used by people in pursuit of excellence in different fields, including different areas of art. They illustrate how the Chinese view achieving a great level of excellence or creativity. It may also explain why many parents encourage, and often push, their children to practise various forms of the arts, such as playing a musical instrument, painting, Chinese calligraphy and Chinese chess, as a means of achieving artistic creativity. Even today, the Chinese believe that people will not achieve high levels of excellence and creativity unless they attain a certain level of skill. Therefore, the training of basic skills is important for the cultivation of creativity.

This belief in the pursuit of excellence through hard work also implies that the Chinese notion of creativity in many ways equals perfection and excellence, resulting in the kind of achievement that adds a significant contribution to the field they have chosen to pursue. So it may be very similar to the Big-C—the extreme form of creativity or originality. This can be seen in the studies of implicit theories of creativity. The Chinese people like to identify characteristics such as 'contributing to society', 'inspiring other people' and 'appreciated by other people'. Here, creativity is valuable only when it is recognized by others. An example to illustrate this point is the famous sentence written by a distinguished poet, Du Fu (杜甫, 712–70), who wrote about his way of pursuing literary creativity by writing poetry. The original sentence was,

'My peculiarity is perfecting sentences, and I will never stop until I reach those surprising lines' (为人性僻耽佳句，语不惊人死不休) (Du, *Jiangshangzhi*). Here, the poet is pursuing the goal of composing 'surprising lines' which no one has used before. This sentence is often used to describe how Chinese view creativity.

This last feature of Chinese creativity may well explain the fanaticism for creativity in China in the twenty-first century. Acknowledging a deficiency in creativity as a 'cultural problem', the Chinese tend to take a proactive approach to 'solving' those problems, and are optimistic about the future. There are enough scientific research and popular books in the West, addressing the issue of how easily creativity can be diminished by various human efforts (namely outside incentives). We know very little about how to enhance— effectively and deliberately—creativity in school and other social settings. Creativity is somehow viewed as an exquisite trait and should be dealt with delicately. The Chinese notion of creativity, however, stresses more on potential growth. We should not be surprised if one day deliberate creativity training and education become part of the regular curriculum in China. Clearly, more research needs to be done to examine whether there is indeed an effective way to promote one's creativity through deliberate training in a persistent and concentrated fashion. Nevertheless, our understanding of creativity would be greatly enriched if we were to integrate knowledge gained from other cultures. Just as China has taken advantage of learning from the West, the world too can benefit considerably from learning the values and experience from Chinese societies, both past and present.

References

Allan, S. 2003. 'The Great One, Water, and the Laozi: New Light from Guodian.' *T'oung Pao* 89 (4–5): 237–85. The Netherlands: BRILL.

Amabile, T.M. 1983. *The Social Psychology of Creativity.* New York: Springer-Verlag.

―――. 1996. *Creativity in Context: Update to The Social Psychology of Creativity.* Boulder, CO: Westview Press.

Ames, R. 2005. 'Collaterality in Early Chinese Cosmology: An Argument for Confucian Harmony as Creatio In Situ'. *Taiwan Journal of East Asian Studies* 2 (1): 43–70.

Ames, R., and D. Hall. 2001. *Focusing the Familiar: A Translation and Philosophical Interpretation of the Zhongyong.* Honolulu: University of Hawaii Press.

Berthrong, J. 1998. *Concerning Creativity: A Comparison of Chu Hsi, Whitehead, and Neville.* Albany. NY: State University of New York Press.

Cai, X. 2006. *A Selected Collection of the Analects.* Beijing: Huaxia Publishing House.

Chan, D.W., and L.K. Chan. 1999. 'Implicit Theories of Creativity: Teachers' Perception of Student Characteristics in Hong Kong.' *Creativity Research Journal* 12 (3): 185–95.

Chang, C. 1970. *Creativity and Taoism: A Study of Chinese Philosophy, Art and Poetry*. (1st Harper paperback ed.). New York: Harper & Row.

Csikszentmihalyi, M. 1988. 'Society, Culture, and Person: A Systems View of Creativity.' In *The Nature of Creativity: Contemporary Psychological Perspectives*, edited by R.J. Sternberg, 325–39. New York: Cambridge University Press.

———. 1996. *Creativity: Flow and the Psychology of Discovery and Invention*. New York: HarperCollins.

———. 1999. 'Implications of a Systems Perspective for the Study of Creativity.' In *Handbook of Creativity*, edited by R.J. Sternberg. Cambridge: Cambridge University Press.

Eckstein, A., J.K. Fairbank and L.S. Yang. 1960. 'Economic Change in Early Modern China: An Analytical Framework.' *Economic Development and Cultural Change* 9 (1): 1–29.

Fingarette, H. 1983. 'The Music of Humanity in the Conversations of Confucius.' *Journal of Chinese Philosophy* 10 (4): 331–56.

Gardner, H. 1989. 'The Key in the Slot: Creativity in a Chinese Key.' *Journal of Aesthetic Education* 23 (1): 141–58.

———. 1993. *The Creators of the Modern Era*. New York: Basic Books.

———. 1996. 'The Creators' Patterns.' In *Dimensions of Creativity*, edited by M.A. Boden. Cambridge: MIT Press.

Graham, A.C. 1989. *Disputers of the Tao: Philosophical Argument in Ancient China*. Chicago: Open Court.

Guilford, J.P. 1956. 'Structure of Intelligence.' *Psychological Bulletin* 53: 267–93.

Helsen, R. 1996. 'In Search of the Creative Personality.' *Creativity Research Journal* 9 (4): 295–306.

Jiang, Z. 2000. *On Science and Technology*. Beijing: Central Party Literature Press.

Khatena, J. 2003. *Enhancing Creativity of Gifted Children: A Guide for Parents and Teachers*. Translated by Z. Kai, W. Wang and Y. Xu. Shanghai: Shanghai Translation. (Original work published 2000).

Kim, K.H. 2005. 'Learning from Each Other: Creativity in East Asian and American Education.' *Creativity Research Journal* 17: 337–47.

———. 2007. 'Exploring the Interactions between Asian Culture (Confucianism) and Creativity.' *Journal of Creative Behavior* 41: 28–54.

Kim, K.H., H. Lee, K. Chae, L. Andersen and C. Lawrence. 2011. 'Creativity and Confucianism among American and Korean Educators.' *Creativity Research Journal* 23: 357–71.

Kuo, Y.Y. 1996. 'Taoistic Psychology of Creativity.' *Journal of Creative Behavior* 30 (3): 197–212.

Li, J. 1997. 'Creativity in Horizontal and Vertical Domains'. *Creativity Research Journal*, 10, 107–32.

Lin, Y. 1935/2010. *My Country and My People*. Benediction Classics.

Montgomery, D., K.S. Bull and L. Balche. 1993. 'Characteristics of the Creative Person.' *American Behavioral Scientist* 37 (1): 68–78.

Mou Zongsan Xian Sheng Quan Ji. (Complete Works of Mou Zongsan). Taipei: Student Books, 31: 39.

Needham, J. 1956. *Science and Civilization in China.* vol. 2: History of Scientific Thought. Cambridge, UK: Cambridge University Press.

Niu, W. 2006. 'Development of Creativity Research in Chinese Societies: A Comparison of Mainland China, Taiwan, Hong Kong, and Singapore.' In *The International Handbook of Creativity*, edited by J.C. Kaufman and R.J. Sternberg, 374–94. New York: Cambridge University Press.

————. 2012. 'Confucian Ideology and Creativity.' *The Journal of Creative Behavior* 46 (4): 274–84.

Niu, W., and D. Liu. 2009. 'Enhancing Creativity: A Comparison between Effects of an Indicative Instruction to be Creative and a More Elaborate Heuristic Instruction on Chinese Student Creativity.' *Psychology of Aesthetics, Creativity, and the Arts* 3 (2): 93–98.

Niu, W., and R.J. Sternberg. 2002. 'Contemporary Studies on the Concept of Creativity: The East and the West.' *Journal of Creative Behavior* 36: 269–88.

————. 2006. 'The Philosophical Roots of Western and Eastern Conceptions of Creativity.' *Journal of Theoretical and Philosophical Psychology* 26: 1001–21.

Ng, A.K. 2000. *Why Asians Are Less Creative than Westerners.* Upper Saddle River, NJ: Prentice Hall.

Peng, W., and J.A. Plucker. 2012. 'Recent Transformations in China's Economic, Social, and Education Policies for Promoting Innovation and Creativity.' *Journal of Creative Behavior* 46 (4): 247–73.

Rudowicz, E. 2003. 'Creativity and Culture, a Two-way Interaction.' *Scandinavian Journal of Educational Research* 47 (3): 273–90.

——. 2004. 'Creativity among Chinese People: Beyond the Western Perspective.' In *Creativity: When East Meets West*, edited by S. Lau, A. Hui and G.Y.C. Ng, 55–86. Hackensack, NJ: World Scientific Publishing.

Rudowicz, E., and A. Hui. 1996. 'Creativity and a Creative Person: Hong Kong Perspective.' *Australasian Journal of Gifted Education* 5 (2): 5–11.

——. 1997. 'The Creative Personality: Hong Kong Perspective.' *Social Behavior and Personality* 12 (1): 139–57.

——. 1998. 'Hong Kong Chinese People's Views of Creativity.' *Gifted Education International* 13 (2): 159–74.

Rudowicz, E., and X.D. Yue. 2000. 'Concepts of Creativity: Similarities and Differences among Mainland, Hong Kong, and Taiwanese Chinese.' *Journal of Creative Behavior* 34 (3): 175–92.

Runco, M.A. 1990. 'Implicit Theories and Ideational Creativity.' In *Theories of Creativity*, edited by M.A. Runco and R.S. Albert Newbury Park, CA: Sage.

Runco, M.A., and M.D. Bahleda. 1987. 'Implicit Theories of Artistic, Scientific and Everyday Creativity.' *Journal of Creative Behavior* 20: 93–98.

Runco, M.A., D.J. Johnson and P.K. Bear. 1993. 'Parents' and Teachers' Implicit Theories of Children's Creativity.' *Child Study Journal* 23 (2): 91–113.

Schwartz, B.I. 1985. *The World of Thought in Ancient China.* Cambridge: Belknap Press of Harvard University.

Simonton, D.K. 1991. 'Emergence and Realization of Genius: The Lives and Works of 120 Classical Composers.' *Journal of Personality and Social Psychology* 61: 829–40.

———. 1996. 'Individual Genius and Cultural Configurations: The Case of Japanese Civilization.' *Journal of Cross-Cultural Psychology* 27: 354–75.

———. 2000. 'Creativity: Cognitive, Personal, Developmental, and Social Aspects.' *American Psychologist* 55 (1): 151–58.

Sternberg, R.J. 1985. 'Implicit Theories of Intelligence, Creativity and Wisdom.' *Journal of Personality and Social Psychology* 49: 607–27.

———. 1988. 'A Three-faced Model of Creativity.' In *The Nature of Creativity*, edited by R.J. Sternberg. Cambridge: Cambridge University Press.

Sternberg, R.J., and T.I. Lubart. 1991. 'An Investment Theory of Creativity and Its Development.' *Human Development* 34 (1): 1–31.

———. 1995. *Defying the Crowd: Cultivating Creativity in a Culture of Conformity.* New York: Free Press.

———. 1999. 'The Concept of Creativity: Prospects and Paradigms.' In *Handbook of Creativity*, edited by R.J. Sternberg. 3–15. New York: Cambridge University Press.

Sundararaja, L. 2004. 'Twenty-four Poetic Moods: Poetry and Personality in Chinese Aesthetics.' *Creativity Research Journal* 16 (2–3): 201–14.

Torrance, E.P. 1966. *The Torrance Tests of Creative Thinking: Technical Norms Manual* (Research edition). Princeton, NJ: Personnel Press.

————. 1988. 'The Nature of Creativity as Manifested in Testing.' In *The Nature of Creativity*, edited by R.J. Sternberg. Cambridge: Cambridge University Press.

Tu, W. 1989. 'The Rise of Industrial East Asia: The Role of Confucian Values.' *Copenhagen Papers in East and Southeast Asian Studies* 4: 81–97.

Wang, H. 2005. *Quan Nao Chao Neng Chuang Zao Li* (Whole Brain Super Creative). Xi-An: Shaanxi Normal University Educational Publishing House.

Weber, M. 1951. *The Religion of China: Confucianism and Taoism.* Translated by H.H. Gerth. New York: Free Press/Glencoe, III. (Original work published 1915).

Wen, H. 2009. *Confucian Pragmatism as the Art of Contextualizing Personal Experience and World.* Lanham, MD: Rowman & Littefield.

Yang, Z.F. 2009. *How to Understand the Chinese People: The Collection of Individual and Culture.* Chongqing: Chongqing University Press.

Freud's Creativity: A Pearl Both Born and Harvested at a Great Price

Patrick J. Mahony

In this chapter, which could be titled 'Looking Back to the Present', I wish to trace my personal history that led to my becoming a psychoanalyst, and to my ever-increasing fascination with Freud's creativity. No doubt surprisingly, I shall begin by broaching Katharine Boo's recent powerful book on a Mumbai slum, *Behind the Beautiful Forevers: Life, Death, and Hope in a Mumbai Undercity.*

Again and again, reviewers have highlighted her bracing prose, scrupulous reportage and unfailing empathetic observation of the unfortunate. I was deeply moved by her book because I spent nearly thirty years of my life in a South Bronx slum which, in some ways, was even worse than the fate of the wretched in Mumbai. The Bronx slum ranked as the most dangerous place in United States; most of my childhood friends eventually died of drugs, were murdered, or imprisoned for life—one of whom was my very first playmate—for double homicide. Daily life shuddered under its bedevilled inventory: squalor, smells of rot, addictions; the mentally ill, of whom there were many (including my uneducated but brilliant mother); the benumbed crowding of the poor, the poorer and the poorest of those; everyday armed fights which were accepted as inevitable as rain; the despair of those whose dreams were born and died in their sleep; and the unpredictable calamity of fires set by victims trying to cope with their impotence. For another thing, there abounded the precocious ageing of those who seemed witlessly given to sacrifice necessities for luxuries, a dissonance somewhat tempered by D.H. Lawrence's aphorism that 'The human soul needs actual beauty more than bread'. Last, but not least, the slum-dwellers who justly harboured a suspicion of higher authorities with their removed herd mentality and their benevolent pronouncements. Indeed, seemingly creative efforts by national or international organizations can never fully work, for, as all the impoverished will tell you, if what is given is not given with love, over time they will hate you.

For the purpose at hand, though, my main attention is drawn to another feature of Boo's *Behind the Beautiful Forevers* which, I propose, dazzled her reviewers, though it was not singled out by them: the constant entrepreneurial creativity carried out by many slum-dwellers to stave off lurking starvation. On the distant horizons, creativity researchers in their labs and allied professors at their desks can hardly be aware of how fomenting poverty—whether in Mumbai, the Bronx or elsewhere—is a Petri dish which serves to culture creativity in its many guises. Finding ways to survive spurs inventiveness just as much as finding ways to live. Notwithstanding its apparent uniformity to outsiders, a slum is replete with variety. I speak personally: inhabitants of the South Bronx slum actually divide it into the northern, middle and southern parts, of which the last—where I lived—was the most precarious of all. Then, within that southernmost part, streets were distinguished by their relative risks and advantages; relative security and luxury were attributed to the upper, middle and lower parts of each street; and on an ever-reducing scale, the upper, the middle and the lower floors of the tenement houses on each street were similarly ranked. The whole was unpredictably criss-crossed by the thuggery of turf domination. Along with all that, positive creativity was challenged by the ingenuities of destructive creativity, as is evidenced even today by the mind-boggling histories of torture.

The long story of how I managed to go directly from the depths of hell to become a Fulbright scholar at the

Sorbonne is not relevant here, but a few ancillary details deserve mention. Speaking about his early, relatively improvident life, Freud accurately stated that one never forgets one's childhood experience of poverty. I would add the following: the poor person who rises above his class experiences language differently. In a kind of bilingualism, he never forgets that the language he speaks always has a set of earlier references. That complexity overdetermined my obtaining a doctorate in literature with two theses on major creative writers in the Renaissance, and then becoming a university professor. But alas! Changed circumstances gradually rendered counterproductive the rigid personality structure which had enabled my escape from the slums. A successful personal analysis reopened my creative potential and spurred my desire to become an analyst. I went on to author a lot on Freud as a creative thinker in many fields, ranging from psychoanalysis itself to literature, and I also published a trilogy on Freud the clinician, informed by the truism that the carrying out of psychoanalytic treatment is also an art.

In my new profession, I tempered my aforesaid, longstanding, entrenched suspicion of authority by integrating it with St Thomas Aquinas's philosophically creative procedure: He who searches for the truth must begin by doubting well, *bene dubitare*, the small word bene or well obviating any irresponsible recourse to reckless scepticism. I was always mindful that a true appraisal of Freud's creativity involved contending with the quasi-official idealization of him in the psychoanalytic community. Idealization jars with a reality-based admiration and actually constitutes continuity with demonization in that they both deny humanness. Furthermore, an idealization of Freud correspondingly undercuts his greatness by obfuscating the mixed picture of his struggles and mistakes, which were sometimes severe. To take one example: no longer held to secrecy, I take this occasion to make public for the first time a devastating truth about Freud's most famous case history of the so-called Wolf Man. With the treatment of some four years ending in a serious impasse, Freud imposed a forced termination. According to the received appraisal of Freud's technical gesture, it brilliantly precipitated some important interpretative data at the end. In actuality—as I was told by two establishment analysts who were closely involved with Freud's patient over many years—Freud accepted him into analysis on condition that he would first have his pregnant girlfriend undergo an abortion. While in analysis, the Wolf Man married her, but alas! They never succeeded in having a child, and the traumatized Wolf Man never forgave Freud for that narcissistic blow. In that light, Freud's forced termination was in fact a repetitive compulsion of the forced pregnancy he had occasioned at the beginning.

In the spirit of a balanced appraisal and a negotiation between what is known, ill-known and unknown, my essay is divided into three parts: a rehearsal of Freud's well-merited attributes and achievements which have contributed to the betterment of society; next, a disarming discussion of Freud's negative attitudes that would appear to undermine the possibility of any cultural contribution; and lastly, an examination of Freud's general as well as specific responses to his creative crux. I should add that a sub-motif runs throughout my exposition: a mainstream reaction to Freud which actually undermines a genuine appreciation of his creative accomplishments.

A litany of Freud's glorious creative achievements

Freud belongs to the list of the select few great creators whose ideas have transformed the world. Fittingly, his creativity has elicited praise from numerous leading scholars, even from various domains tangential to psychoanalysis proper. We are fortunate that the available data on Freud comprises the most pertinent and incisive information on any one individual which has ever been amassed; that precious information enables us to follow Freud's creative development. After benefiting from a classical education, the young Freud had the fortune to be trained by some of the greatest scientific minds, who themselves were caught up in the creative fermentation running across so many disciplines. Yet Freud readily admitted that he was a late bloomer and did not count within that circle of great precocious thinkers. To his Viennese colleagues, he lauded Nietzsche's precocity: 'That Nietzsche raised questions about the origin of evil already as a boy of thirteen is in keeping with the fact that other great thinkers and discoverers also established their life tasks at about that age: at eleven years of age, Jean-François Champillion, the pioneering decipherer of Egyptian hieroglyphs, set himself the task which he solved some twenty-five years later.' Compared to Picasso who manifested his prodigious powers by the age of seven, and Einstein who made many of his revolutionary discoveries before the age of thirty, Freud was indeed a late bloomer, manifesting his world-shaking ability only after he reached forty years of age, after which he did not stop.

But precocity is one thing, and early academic proficiency and creative versatility are another. In a comparative study of seven modern creators, including Einstein, Picasso and T.S. Eliot, Howard Gardner concluded that Freud was 'probably the one with the greatest academic strengths', with the most marked 'ambition and self-confidence', and the one who could have left his mark in other areas too. More than that, Freud stands out among his contemporaries as the one who made the greatest cultural impact; no scientist can match up to Freud's influence on art and literature. In the history of ideas, 'it would be hard to find someone whose influence was so immediate, so broad, and so deep', but most importantly, Freud ranks among the limited number of those outstanding creative thinkers who have given the world a new and profound paradigm. 'Perhaps only Aristotle and Darwin have equalled Freud's marriage of theory and observation in the broad realm of the life sciences.' Freud also went on to found a school which was a revival of the Graeco-Roman type of philosophical schools, which have no parallel in modern times and which constituted a remarkable event in the history of modern culture. In his dedication to all those endeavours, let it be said that Freud's preoccupation was not with glory but with scientific advancement. He would have agreed with John Updike's definition of celebrity as a mask that eats into the face.

Although many of Freud's creative achievements have been criticized, he is almost universally admired as a writer. There is a deep level of meaning to Freud's writing; more than just a working medium, it was for him a personally, as well as professionally, organizing, and creative experience. He would have agreed with St Augustine, who said: 'Admittedly, therefore, I try to count myself among those who write as they progress and who progress as they write.' Essential to both his professional and personal identity, Freud wrote constantly—finished pre-analytic and psychoanalytic treatises, drafts, travel journals, visitors' books, diaries, copious notes, chronological records, translations and a mountainous correspondence. Although he destroyed large quantities of his manuscripts at least three times in his life (in 1885, 1907 and 1938), what remains of his literary production is impressive. If we were to take the estimated 14,000 extant letters out of the some 20,000 which Freud wrote, and if each were edited to occupy an average of a page and a half in print, we would have an edition of 21,000 pages, or more than three times the length of The Standard Edition of the Complete Psychological Works of Sigmund Freud. A dream awaiting tomorrow's tomorrow, the complete publication of Freud's extant work would easily comprise some 150 volumes. When we bear this in mind, we quickly realize that he numbers among the small circle of great prolific writers through all history. No other scientific author, one might add, has matched Freud's communicative power. Freud is not only one of the foremost prose writers in German literature but also one of the greatest persuasive writers in world literature.

Apart from his creativity as a theoretician and as a writer, Freud manifested his inventiveness, though in a very mixed way, in his role as a clinician. To Socrates's time-honoured counsel to know yourself, Freud added the historical correction: 'You can know yourself only through another.' For that purpose, Freud (whose first name, Sigmund, literally means victory mouth) invented what is reductively called a talking cure. He invented a plurivocal, or more specifically, a quadrivocal cure, a fact which is overlooked in the appreciation of Freud's creativity. Whatever has been said, heard, written or read in the life of humanity can be categorized into four basic kinds of discourses. For the first and only time in the history of the literary genre or social ritual, the four basic discourses of necessity appear together, and that happens in the analytic setting. The interaction between those four discourses, moreover, constitutes one of the ways to describe analytic success. Unfortunately—starting even with Freud himself—the rich discursive nature of the analytic treatment continues to be ignored.

Perilous cracks in the pearl

The wealth of Freud's creative abilities intensified his affect-laden imbroglio about the very discipline he founded. If Galileo, Darwin and Einstein braved the world in proposing unusual truths about external reality, Freud's onerous lot was to propose even more unwelcome truths about our inner reality. For example, 'Psychoanalysis is the first major scientific theory of which an integral part has been a historical vision of precisely how that theory should have arisen in its author's own mind.' And yet, although—in a gesture of self-heroization—Freud exaggerated the external opposition his theories encountered, mainstream psychoanalytic literature, while registering approval of Freud's account, correspondingly minimized the internal obstacles he experienced from his own psyche. The startling fact, however, is that Freud, the monumental benefactor of humankind, was deeply at odds with it and also with the very therapeutic discipline he founded. On an a priori basis, his deep-rooted negative attitudes would even seem to obviate any cultural contributions on his part.

I begin with Freud's state of mind about his own profession. While following his life's dominant aim of achieving philosophical knowledge, Freud regarded clinical sessions as a necessary—although imperfect—laboratory for his research. The early Freud commented to his intimate friend Wilhelm Fliess: 'As a young man I knew no longing other than for philosophical knowledge, and now I am about to fulfil it as I move from medicine to psychology. I became a therapist against my will.' Much later, in *The Question of Lay Analysis*, he confessed, 'My self-knowledge tells me that I have never really been a doctor in the proper sense. I became a doctor through being compelled to deviate from my original purpose; and the triumph of my life lies in my having, after a long and roundabout journey, found my way back to my earliest path.' And then Freud went on to admit, 'I have no knowledge of having had in my early years any craving to help suffering humanity.'

When we narrow our focus and attend next to Freud's attitude toward his patients, we find that he was concerned for their welfare only as a means of both earning a living and learning. Four evidential examples among many will suffice:

- 'Only a few patients are worth the trouble we spend on them, so that we are not allowed to have a therapeutic attitude, but we must be glad to have learned something in every case.'
- 'The patients are disgusting and are giving me an opportunity for new studies on technique.'
- Concerning a female patient who dropped out of analysis, Freud wrote to Jung: 'Of course, she is right [to stop her analysis], because she is beyond any possibility of therapy, but it is still her duty to sacrifice herself to science.'
- Sándor Ferenczi, one of Freud's most entrusted colleagues and a member of the Secret Committee, painfully recorded this pertinent experience in his private journal: 'I do remember some of Freud's remarks that he let slip in my presence, obviously counting on my discretion, namely: "Patients are rabble . . . They are no good, except to make a living from and to give material to learn from. "''

We can better understand Freud's ambivalence towards his profession and his patients when we see it within the larger context of his contempt for his fellow men in general. As the sociologist Philip Rieff said, Freud did not show any awareness of the ancient refinements in democratic theory and its distinctions between 'people' and 'mob'. Freud frequently called his fellow humans *Gesindel* (trash, rabble). That social contempt was not a casual or rare judgement. Far from it: Freud privately voiced the leitmotif of his social contempt throughout his pre-analytic and analytic life—as a teenager, then as a young adult, as a middle-aged and an elderly analyst. It mattered not whether Freud was speaking to friends, male and female. The accumulated weight indicates that his socially contemptuous reflections cannot be totally dismissed as expressions of momentary exasperation.

Because the subject of Freud's misanthropy has been so controversial, I shall rely on direct citation rather than paraphrase any of the abounding evidence. From over two dozen quotations, I have chosen a representative sampling in which Freud addresses five colleagues:

- 'I have found little that is "good" about human beings on the whole. In my experience most of them are trash.'
- 'The unworthiness of human beings, including the analysts, always has impressed me deeply, but why

should analysed men and women be better? Analysis makes for integration but does not of itself make for goodness.'

- 'In the depths of my being I remain convinced that my dear fellow creatures—with few exceptions—are a wretched lot.'
- 'I must admit that the rabble who read these things [of self-confession in the dream book] don't deserve a shred of honesty.'
- 'The care that weighs me down about the future I can best convey to you genetically. It comes from the time when psychoanalysis depended on me alone, and when I was so uneasy about what the human rabble would make out of it when I was no longer alive.'

I should briefly add that Freud's social disdain played an unrecognized role in his creative expression. In *Die Traumdeutung*, Freud disclosed this private secret: 'My emotional life has always insisted that I should have an intimate friend and a hated enemy.' Freud inscribed that dynamic in many of his writings, where he imagined a dialogue with his readership divided into friendly believers and hostile objectors. Throughout the years, this dialogic feature has engaged Freud's readers and even pleased them. But there is a different story behind the scenes, as it were. Only while writing his text could Freud the all-powerful author enjoy controlling his audience.

Like many other authors, Freud became depressed after he finished writing. But the additional element in his depression was that once he published his writing to the outside world, he could no longer control or stage-manage the responses of his real readers. Those readers were now part of the general world he so mistrusted, and he felt helpless before the possibility of their dismissive, even castrating, reactions.

Freud's creative crux and his general solution

How could Freud persist in his gigantic efforts that brought relief to so many, and yet be dismissive of them at the same time? How can we understand better what may be called the imperilled pearl, his creativity? Before answering these questions, let us further state that Freud's creative crux lay in his negative attitudes which themselves were magnified by what he perceived as the difficulties intrinsic to psychoanalysis. He did not shy away from revealing that psychoanalysis emerged as an impossible profession, for it was unnatural for both the analyst and the patient. Freud insisted, and I quote, 'There is nothing for which man's capabilities are less suited than psychoanalysis.' Complicating the natural resistance of humankind to psychoanalysis was Freud's far-reaching pessimism that increased even more after he became a psychoanalyst. As he confided to Lou-Andreas Salomé: 'I cannot be an optimist, and I believe I differ from the pessimists only in that wicked, stupid, senseless things don't upset me, because I have accepted them from the beginning as part of what the world is made of.'

Along a similar vein of thought, Freud imagined civilization as originating in a primal murder; he looked upon common moral codes as possible threats, not solutions, to psychic health; and he envisaged a fundamental drive to be one of death. He also saw that, like the tragic Oedipus, we are in exile—especially when most at home—and that our escape from such a domestic dilemma is through the pass of the superego. In Freud's vision, the superego is an *inneres Ausland*—an internal foreign territory—whereby we are even further exiled, displaced in the home of our very selves. As if this domestic exile were not enough, Freud gave it a temporal dimension: he believed that 'the past, the traditions of the race and of the people, lives on in the ideologies of the super-ego.' How then can we ever be at home with ourselves? Not merely through the Delphic counsel of knowing yourself, Freud would contend. In his innovative version of the oracle, to know yourself can be known only through another, but that other's analysis, Freud memorably insisted, is also interminable.

The aforementioned pervasive attitude of professional and social scorn and pessimism would have had a deadening effect on creativity in some lesser spirits. And what was the effect on Freud? At first glance, the measure to which he succeeded or not can be related to his double thesis that mental health involves the cornerstone of our humanity—the ability 'to work and to love'. If, for a moment, we disassociate work from love, we may further ask, how did Freud manage to accomplish so much? The Chinese thinker Confucius once said that if you were to find a job that fully suited you, you would never have to work again. As we shall see, that maxim does not quite fit Freud who nevertheless super-invested in a life of work. At the best of times, Freud was driven to spend a larger part of the day in intellectual work. For example, a month before the appearance of *Studies on Hysteria*, Freud described his need for a Goethe-like demon this way: 'A man like me cannot live without a hobby-horse, without a consuming passion, without— in Schiller's words—a tyrant. I have found one. In its service I know no limits.' In an earlier letter to his friend, Oskar Pfister, we read, perhaps, Freud's finest depiction of his single-minded dedication to work—'a free play of the imagination'—which he would like to enjoy up to the very moment of death:

> I cannot face with comfort the idea of life without work; work and the free play of the imagination are for me the same thing, I take no pleasure in anything else. . . . I have

one quite secret prayer: that I may be spared any wasting way and crippling of my ability to work because of physical deterioration.

Let us understand, however, that Freud did not consider his hours with patients as work per se. He declared to Karl Abraham, 'I have to recuperate from psychoanalysis by working, otherwise I could not endure it.'

Yet, despite Freud's total commitment to work, complete psychic freedom and relaxation eluded him. To various friends he acknowledged that he needed some measure of physical or psychic pain, not just for working, but for *Leistung*, working well, achieving. As such, Freud differed from Tagore in his creative melancholy and even more from Jacques Derrida (personal communication) who enjoyed himself while writing his many books and articles. Freud contended that 'Unpleasure remains the sole means of education.' His greatest period of creativity, in fact, was attended by serious, prolonged discomfort, which he partly relieved by his self-destructive addiction to nicotine. Painful work could also serve to contain other suffering. Thus, when the death of his favourite grandson caused him great grief, Freud wrote to Pfister with a similar message about stoic commitment to work: 'I do as much work as I can, and am grateful for the distraction. The loss of a child seems to be a grave blow to one's narcissism; as for mourning, that will no doubt come later.

Let us now consider the factor of love which we had momentarily separated in Freud's conjoined programme of work and love. He defined the other side of his idealistic programme this way: 'During my whole life I have endeavoured to uncover truths. I had no other intention and everything else was completely a matter of indifference to me. My single motive was the love of truth.' Notice his particular qualification: the love of truth. What is most telling is that Freud often spoke of the love of truth (*Wahrheitsliebe*)—seventeen times in his *Gesammelte Werke*—but never once did he mention its inverse, the truth of love. Moreover, he did not deal with the double dynamic of prior knowledge as necessary for love and a consequent love affording knowledge not obtainable otherwise.

The theoretical limitations just mentioned are echoed in a letter which Freud sent to Romain Rolland. Strangely, Freud, too, claimed the title of 'apostle of love' for himself, but let us listen to how Freud defined it in a stark utilitarian fashion:

> I was myself a disciple of the love of mankind, not from
> sentimental motives or in pursuit of an ideal, but for sober,

economic reasons, because our inborn instincts and the world around us being what they are, I could not but regard that love as no less essential for the survival of the human race than for such things as technology.

In this bizarre statement which mocks all well-balanced libidinal involvement, Freud wants to champion love of truth as his ideal, although he justifies his love of his fellow beings not on idealistic grounds but on empirical ones. In short, love and work constituted in Freud's mind a disharmonious asymmetry.

Freud's creative crux and his gendered response

If we train Freud's general theory of love on to women, we come upon what can be graphically described as his adamantine contention with different figures of Eve. Abundant scholarship has made familiar Freud's raw depreciation of women, as is evident in this passage:

> [Woman's] superego is never so inexorable, so impersonal, so independent of its emotional origins as we require it to be in men . . . they show less sense of justice than man . . . they are less ready to submit to the great exigencies of life . . . they are more often influenced in their judgements by feelings of affection or hostility.

Elsewhere, Freud could depart from a direct, negative statement and, to some degree, erotically sublimate his attitude to women in a sustained imaginative act. In effect, Freud conceived of the divinized power of his 'Logos' so as to be able to contend in a largely successful way with the combined Oedipal mother as well as the kindly, nourishing pre-Oedipal mother. Freud's masterpiece, *Die Traumdeutung*, best shows this eroticized textuality. Here is Freud sexualizing the dream:

> Every dream has at least one place . . . a navel as it were, by which it joins with the unknown. . . . Then this is the dream's navel (*der Nabel*), the place at which it straddles the unknown.

We note that the dreamer joins with, and even straddles, the mother, the unknown. The suggestiveness of Freud's description is amplified by the fact that the word 'unknown' in German comes from a verb (*erkennen*) which, like the English 'know', can be used in the Biblical sense of carnal knowledge. There is more. Freud not only sexualized the dream but also sexualized his prolonged exposition of it. Thus he pictured his whole investigation of the dream as a symbolically charged journey through nature. Its landscape, he explained, symbolized the female genitalia, and its woods symbolized the mother. Here's a sampling of that erotic symbolism which illustrates Freud's investigative wandering:

> When, after passing through a narrow defile, we suddenly emerge upon a piece of high ground where the path divides and the finest prospects open up on every side . . . such is the case with us, now that we have surmounted the first interpretation of a dream. Having followed one path to its end, we may now retrace our steps and choose another starting point for our rambles through the problems of dream-life.

Briefly, in his scientific masterpiece, Freud wedded his epistemological exposition to an exploration of the maternal body, Oedipal and pre-Oedipal. As such, *Die Traumdeutung* must count not only as a scientific treatise and an autobiography; its underlying textuality must be partly seen as an erotic prose poem.

If one concept of woman was more or less worked through and symbolically integrated into the overall text of *Die Traumdeutung*, another kind of woman eluded Freud. If the pre-Oedipal mother was kind and nurturing, she could also be feared for her imagined archaic power and destructiveness. That mother in Freud's psyche was not subjected to a working through (*Durcharbeitung*). Her greater meaning for him perdured, mostly unconsciously, symbolized by America. And therein lies one of the strangest stories from the life of any eminent creator.

While Freud changed his mind on many topics, he never altered his vehement anti-Americanism which came from the depths of his being. Incomparably more than the anti-Americanism of his continental contemporaries, America haunted Freud and aroused his bitterness. That identification was above and beyond what he thought of women in general. Like an invasive virus which pops up everywhere on a computer, she appeared throughout Freud's writing, everywhere, as an undeveloped, monotonous marker. The rampant dispersal of the pre-Oedipal mother in Freud's textuality substituted for concentrated grappling with her on his part. Thus, no matter which genre Freud wrote in—scientific treatise, dialogue, history, biography, autobiography, private letters, case-history narratives—America came to his mind as a ready example of what was bad. And no matter which subject Freud discussed—dreams, clinical theory, psychoanalytic treatment, history or social issues— America emerged as an immediate association of what was bad. Her omnipresence throughout the gamut of the most diverse communicative occasions does indicate that Freud was in fact not freely associating; the return of the repressed appeared as he was compulsively associating— wherever, whenever, to whomever.

If, in Freud's view, women in general were a dark continent, then pre-Oedipal, matriarchal America was the new and darkest continent, a heart of darkness. In the light of his thesis about the Oedipus complex as an acculturating achievement, he was horrified that America was a land in which the primitive woman ruled over 'savages'. We overhear a similar denunciation as Freud railed:

- to an American patient: 'Women rule American society; they are an anti-cultural phenomenon'; and
- to Jung: 'In America, the mother is decided by the dominant member of the family. American culture really is a bottomless abyss; the men have become a flock of sheep and the women play the ravening wolves—within the family circle, of course. I ask myself whether such conditions have ever existed in the world before. I really don't think they have.'

Nowhere in Freud's scientific works can we find the comparable equivalent of America as the ubiquitous presence of the return of the repressed. Commentators on Freud err in concluding that he rarely spoke of the pre-Oedipal mother. The overdetermined fact is that he always spoke of her, though disguised in his symbolic geography. Yet, at the deepest unconscious level, she was irrelevant, for, if America had not existed, Freud would have had to invent her. She functioned as a necessary ingredient in

Freud's psychic economy, partly cathartically siphoning off Freud's manifold conflictual tensions, and thus permitting him—although only to some undefinable extent, a greater creative freedom in grappling with countless issues.

But the most bewitching story is yet to come. In her omnipresence, America could not be contained within Freud's writings. Like an uncontrollable death-goddess, she went on to inscribe herself in his body as text and she destroyed it. This nigh-unbelievable phenomenon began with Freud's only visit to the States in 1909. He believed that his twenty-three-day transatlantic visit undermined his general health forever. To restore it, he went to Karlsbad for an extensive period of three weeks. For the same restorative purpose, I discovered, he had to return there every year for the next six years, after which he could no longer go because of wartime conditions.

But Freud's itemized account of his particular wrecked health is even more bewildering: he mistakenly linked the American visit with the novel onset of his digestive troubles and writer's cramp. He traced his first attack of a recurrent prostatitis to America; he amplified a condition of colitis into a 'definite, though mild attack of appendicitis' in America; and he went on to make the additional lament that his very handwriting 'deteriorated so very much since the American trip'.

Such, then, was America—an anti-cultural, omnipotent mother, a force of nature with magical, destructive powers. Her demonic power was symbolically repressed into a transatlantic embodiment that made Freud regress into an infantile, paranoid state of victimhood. Fortunately, that state did not paralyse his overall creativity, as profound as it was asymmetrical.

As I look back now on my discussion of Freud, I must insist that a demythifying exposure of Freud's social attitudes does not diminish the estimate of his contributions to humankind. Quite the opposite. Based on infantile needs for perfection, prior idealizations of Freud falsely enhance his stature by disregarding what he personally had to overcome. As a matter of fact, a genuine appreciation of him increases when we realize the vast personal conflicts he had to endure in his unwavering dedication to science. Comparing himself to Jacob who limped after battling with the angel, Freud said that he limped after struggling with the unconscious. I would rather say that sometimes he was crippled, but often he could run.

Yet the question stubbornly remains: How in the world was Freud able to found what he in effect labelled the 'impossible' and 'unnatural' discipline of psychoanalysis? Notwithstanding Freud's genius, there were others in history who were brighter than he, and yet they did not come near to discovering the dynamic unconscious. How is that? For a partial answer, I propose the following: there remains the disabusing realization that Freud's monomaniacal preoccupation with the love of knowledge rather than the knowledge of love might have facilitated—if not allowed—his painful journey in discovering psychoanalysis. To put it differently: had Freud been more emotionally engaged with his fellow humans, perhaps he would never have gained the distance necessary for gaining his profound insights into human suffering. We might further explain that Freud was helped by his heroic courage and Goethe-like striving 'in ceaseless toil'. For him, 'what is finest and noblest in men [is] their heroism, their self-sacrifice, their social sense'.

It is very much to the point that Freud attributed his achievements more to his character than to his intellect; and that, within that distinction, he judged that courage—the thought of being a 'fearless human being'—was his pre-eminent character trait. Yet Freud went on to undercut his grand stature by admitting that the unconscious disbelief in death might be the very 'secret of heroism'. While that admission was in itself heroic, it still raises the question as to whether Freud's own heroic courage was based on illusory non-truth. Greatness indeed, and the most radical self-doubt, too. A non-negligible limitation, one may hastily charge. In reply, we may cite the sobering truism in classical ethics that to have one virtue perfectly, a person must have them all perfectly. Is not imperfection the quintessential lot of humankind, including Freud? I hearken back to my paper's all-too-human subtitle: a pearl both born and harvested at great price.

Beyond Freud

My concluding remarks concern the future of studies about creativity and psychoanalysis at large. First of all, I have a lot of reserve about what may be called futurology, given that everyone can claim expertise since all predictions have not yet been disproven, and given the narcissistic tendency to replace reality by one's unfulfilled wishes. The more distant the future, the greater is the risk of overrating one's predictions as truth—a fact seen every day in the fields of meterology and economics. Historically, the greatest lesson for me has been the development of Christianity. If we take the period from 33 AD to 66 AD, Jesus, the divine source of that religion, was crucified, and St James, the subsequent leader of Christians in Jerusalem, was also killed; Peter, Christ's successor, and Paul, the greatest Christian theologian at the time, were killed in Rome; and none of the gospels was yet written. All that was compounded by the difficulty of communication among the extant few thousand Christians dispersed throughout the Roman Empire. Now if we anachronistically imagine a modern historian or a well-informed pollster living in

Rome at the time, he would be tempted to doubt any endurance of the young religion. So much for the lack of guarantee even in doubting well!

Hence I come not to my predictions but to my wishes. Since psychoanalytic treatment aims at psychic integration rather than at large-scale ethical improvement, I wish that it would be supplemented by meditative practice. The French psychoanalyst Francis Pasche accurately stated that the prolonged maintenance of an analyst's neutral stance can only be assured by ascesis, a concept generally taboo in American psychoanalysis. Would the erosion of American power plus a monumental catastrophe make its analysts more disposed to conjoin analytic treatment with meditation, or would that eventuality come from the East with its long history of honouring meditative practice? As it is, I cannot help thinking about what would have happened to Freud and his clinical theories if he had undertaken sustained meditation.

And I wish for a deeper exploration of the ego ideal, a term, according to my own research, used by Freud seventy-one times in the German edition of his works but appearing only five times in its standard English translation (and two of those occurrences have no justification in the German original!). Without doubt, because of his own narcissistic conflicts, Freud did not see clearly, and often confused his groping distinctions between the ideal ego—the oldest and largely unconscious part of the ego—and the largely conscious and much later formation of the ego ideal. While the ideal ego never evolves and is not ordered to reality, the ego ideal is mostly conscious and contains evolving, realizable aspirations. Furthermore, the ideal ego, inheriting the state of primary narcissism, exists as a psychic structure at the most primitive level of the ego, and its grandiose fantasies of omnipotence and omniscience are drive-invested (without the drives, harmless fantasies would arise from that level). Also to be borne in mind is how the ideal ego contributes significantly to the intensification of Oedipal conflicts.

A promising indication of the problems of perfection posed by the ideal ego is found in two complementary insights: for the French existentialist Gabriel Marcel, man is always God with or without God; for the classical psychoanalyst, Ernest Jones, the God-complex exists in all men. Radical self-sufficiency produces a social alienation so well expressed in Jean-Paul Sartre's drama, *Huis Clos*: 'L'enfer, c'est les autres' (Hell is the others). Offering a corrective to the dangers of perfectionism, Nietzsche contended that the gods may die that man might live, and we might add, the false gods in man may die that he might live. It is truly a doubting well, a *bene dubitare*, which may help one avoid the prison of self-absorption.

In the best of outcomes, the ideal ego constitutes the ultimate greenhouse for eventual grand creativity; inversely, the mystic aspirant faces the challenge to descend in a self-purification through and past the barrier of the drive-invested ideal ego. That psychic structure serves as a hub where transformative creative and mystical practices meet, while going in opposite directions; and yet, as we read in the headnote to Rilke's poem 'Wendung', the commonness linking that adversity is that the 'road from inwardness to greatness passes through sacrifice'. To put it briefly: as partly suggested here, a greater investigation of the ideal ego in its grandiose and omnipotent nature leads to a better comprehension of creativity as well as the struggles besetting a spiritual as well as a mystical path, a path that descends into levels of greater and greater self-searing in order to be there—in greater and greater joy—for the other.

Creativity as a Neuroscientific Mystery

Margaret A. Boden

I: Just what sort of mystery is this?

Many people, still under the influence of nineteenth-century Romantic views, believe that creativity is a mystery which is forever beyond the reach of science. They even believe, again echoing Romanticism, that it is a special faculty, confined to a small elite. They are wrong. In fact, creativity—that is, the ability to generate ideas/artefacts that are new, surprising and valuable—is an aspect of human intelligence in general (Boden 2004, 2010). As such, it is rooted both in our material embodiment and in our sociocultural context, and it depends on the brain. In other words, it is an unsolved puzzle for neuroscientists, not an ineluctable mystery essentially beyond their grasp.

A point of clarification, here: Discussions of creativity are often bedevilled by the discussants adopting different meanings of the word 'new'. An idea may be new to the person who has just come up with it, even though it might have occurred to countless other people in the past. Let us call this P-novelty: 'P' for psychological. Alternatively, the idea may be new, so far as is known, to the entire human history. This is H-novelty: 'H' for historical. Depending on which sense of 'new' is involved, a new idea may or may not count as H-creativity. But it always exemplifies P-creativity, of which H-creativity is clearly a special case. From the psychologist's point of view, and from the neuroscientists' perspective too, the fundamental phenomenon which needs to be explained is P-creativity. Examples of H-creativity—some of which are mentioned below—may be especially interesting to us, as intellectually curious human beings. But they are scientifically relevant, primarily as instances of P-creativity: their 'historical' situation is not a matter for neuroscience. If creativity is an unsolved scientific puzzle rather than an occult and ever-enigmatic mystery, it is nevertheless a puzzle that will be very hard to solve. In common parlance, then, it is a 'mystery'.

The air of mystery is strengthened by the fact that introspection rarely helps. Artists, scientists and mathematicians often report that they have no idea how they came up with their valuable new ideas. Some even use this phenomenological fact to suggest that they didn't come up with the novel idea at all: rather, some ultra-human, perhaps divine, power did so. They forget, of course, that creativity is not unique in this regard: introspection doesn't tell us how we form grammatical sentences, nor how we interpret photographs as depicting specific scenes. In general, much more goes on in our minds below the level of consciousness than can ever be accessed by it. (Were that not so, we'd be paralysed by information overload.) Psychology faces 'introspective mystery' in all areas of mental life.

The main difficulty in solving the puzzle of creativity is not—as is also widely believed—that it is unpredictable. Creativity is indeed largely unpredictable, for a number of different reasons (Boden 2004, ch. 9).The most important reason is the enormous complexity and idiosyncrasy of human minds, the detailed contents of which are largely unknown even to the individual concerned.

In one sense, this does put creativity outside the scope of science. However, that is no reason for the scientist to despair, and no reason either to mark creativity off from other, notionally less mysterious, phenomena. For it is not the aim of science to predict individual events, most of which—unlike Joe Bloggs's suicide—are of no interest to us, anyway: we don't *want* physicists to be able to predict the movements of each grain of sand on the beach. (Even if the suicidal thoughts are assigned some statistical probability, this may not be calculated on purely scientific grounds [Meehl 1954].) Occasionally, events can be precisely predicted by science: think of a returning space capsule splashing into the Pacific Ocean with rescue ships already waiting nearby.

Usually, however, they cannot. Science, in general, isn't focused on the prediction of particularities, even though prediction is an important aspect of experimental method. Rather, it seeks to show how events of a certain class are *possible*, and how they are related to other sorts of events, whether actual or merely conceivable (Boden 2006, 7.iii.d).

Accordingly, a neuroscientific explanation of the puzzling phenomenon of creativity would show us *how it is possible* for this still-mysterious phenomenon to occur. The common view that a science of creativity could predict every detail of creative thought, thus making human artists and scientists (and everyday punsters) redundant, is mistaken.

The 'mystery' of creativity, as regards neuroscience, lies not in its unpredictability but in its computational variety.

As outlined in Section II below, there are several different types of creativity, involving distinct sorts of information processing. A satisfactory neuroscience of creativity would have to illuminate each one of those.

'Illumination', here, means significantly more than locating the brain areas involved. Generally, a neuroscientific *explanation* of a psychological phenomenon does not merely tell us which parts of the brain, and/or which neuronal groups, are active when the phenomenon occurs. Crucially, it tells us what the brain cells are doing, where this is understood not in terms of, for instance, chemical changes but in terms of the computations or information processing, which the cells are performing (Boden 2006, ch. 14).

The computational psychologist John Mayhew, when explaining stereopsis, put it like this: 'Finding a cell that recognizes one's grandmother does not tell you very much more than you started with; after all, you know you can recognize your grandmother. What is needed is an answer to how you, or a cell, or anything at all, does it. The discovery of the cell tells one what does it, but not how it can be done' (Mayhew 1983, 214).

Even if the detailed neuronal circuits involved are known, what the circuits are doing may be obscure. The key questions concern what information is received and/or is passed on by the cell or the cell-group, and how it is computed by it. To put it another way, they concern 'how electrical and chemical signals are used in the brain to represent and process information' (Koch and Segev 1989, 1).

The key point of this paper, then, is that we need to know what sort of information processing is involved in creativity, if we are to have any hope of a neuroscientific explanation of it. And the conclusion will be that we are at present within reach of such an explanation only for one type of creativity. The others will be much more difficult nuts for the neuroscientist to crack.

II: The three types of creativity

Creativity can happen in three main ways, only one of which is typically recognized by people trying to analyse it (including those experimental psychologists who specialize in this area). Specifically, creativity may be combinational, exploratory or transformational (Boden 2004, ch. 3–6).

These are distinguished by the sort of psychological processes which are involved in generating a new idea. A satisfactory neuroscientific theory of creativity would need to explain how each of the three types can come about.

Combinational creativity—which is usually the only type recognized in studies/definitions of creativity—

involves the generation of unfamiliar combinations of familiar ideas. In general, it gives rise to a 'statistical' form of surprise, like the one experienced when an outsider wins the Derby. Everyday examples of combinational creativity include visual collage (in advertisements and MTV videos, for instance); a lot of poetic imagery; all types of analogy (verbal, visual or musical); and the unexpected juxtapositions of ideas found in political cartoons in newspapers. Scientific examples include seeing the heart as a pump, or the atom as a solar system.

Exploratory and transformational creativity are different. Unlike the combinational variety, they are both grounded in some previously existing, and culturally accepted, structured style of thinking, or 'conceptual space'. Of course, combinational creativity, too, depends on a shared conceptual base, but this is, potentially, the entire range of concepts and world-knowledge in someone's mind. A conceptual space, or thinking-style, is both more limited and more tightly structured (often, hierarchically). It may be a board game, for example (chess or Go, perhaps), or a class of chemical structures (aromatic molecules, for instance), or a particular type of music or a piece of sculpture.

In exploratory creativity, existing stylistic rules or conventions are used to generate novel structures (ideas or artefacts), whose possibility may or may not have been realized before the exploration took place. To the extent that it was not, the new structure will be not only satisfying but also surprising. A new painting in the impressionist style, a new benzene derivative, or a new fugue or sonnet are all examples. So is the daily generation of new sentences, fitting the grammatical rules of the language in question.

Exploratory creativity can also involve the search for, and testing of, the specific stylistic limits concerned. Just which types of structure can be generated within this space, and which cannot?

Transformational creativity is the most arresting of the three. Indeed, it leads to 'impossibilist' surprise, wherein the novel idea appears to be not merely new, not even merely strange, but 'impossible'. Seemingly, it simply could not have arisen—and yet it did. In such cases, the shocking new idea arose because some defining dimension of the style, or conceptual space, was altered, so that structures which could not be generated before can now be generated. The greater the alteration, and the more fundamental the stylistic dimension concerned, the greater the shock of impossibilist surprise.

For instance, imagine altering the rule of chess which says that pawns can't jump over other pieces: let us suppose that they're now allowed to do this, as knights have always been. The result would be that some games of chess could now be played which were literally impossible before. Or consider the suggestion, new in 1865, that the benzene molecule may be a ring of carbon atoms: a topologically closed string, rather than—like all previously described molecules—an open one. Exploratory creativity then took over, as organic chemists mapped the space of benzene derivatives. They later went on to ask whether the core of some ring-molecules might include five atoms rather than six, and/or atoms of elements other than carbon. Whether one chooses to call those two questions 'exploratory' or 'transformational' is negotiable. The important point is that they were both driven by specific features of the benzene-space which had been explored for some time.

A comparable, and much more recent, example concerns the shocking idea that some carbon molecules may be hollow spheres. The key transformation, here, was to consider atomic bonds forming not just in one spatial dimension—as in a planar sheet of graphene—but in three. What is generally regarded as the key paper was published in 1985 (Kroto et al. 1985). It reported experimental research on carbon vapours heated to thousands of degrees, in which various multi-atom molecules (but mostly the soccer ball C60, or Buckminsterfullerene) formed spontaneously. Subsequent exploratory creativity synthesized many new 'fullerenes' of differing shapes and sizes. These included open-ended or closed tubes (formed when a small percentage of nickel or cobalt atoms was added) which could act as molecule carriers and electronic conductors, thereby providing for a host of novel technological applications. This pioneering work led to a Nobel Prize eleven years later (Smalley 1996).

That work was rightly seen by the Nobel Committee as 'pioneering', not least because of its detail and systematicity (made possible by the team's development of laser instrumentation for measurement). In fact, however, the central 'shocking idea' had been suggested in 1970, by chemists in Japan and in the UK. But it was then considered too bizarre to be accepted (valued) by the scientific community. Moreover, a closely similar idea, envisaging the addition of impurities to a planar network of carbon atoms (and soon pointing out that the resultant hollow molecules might carry other molecules inside them), had been published in the *New Scientist* as early as 1966, but the author had presented this as scientific fantasy rather than serious research (Jones 1966; cf. Jones 1982, 118–19). This example illustrates the difficulty, in many cases, of deciding whether a particular idea really is new, and/or really is valuable.

In general (though less so in literature), transformational creativity is esteemed more highly than the other two varieties. The people whose names are recorded in history books are usually remembered, above all, for changing the accepted style. Typically, the stylistic change meets with initial resistance. And it often takes some time before it is accepted. That's not surprising. For, transformational creativity 'by definition' involves the breaking/ignoring of culturally sanctioned rules.

However, novel transformations are relatively rare. All artists and scientists spend most of their working time engaged in combinational and/or exploratory creativity. That's abundantly clear when one visits a painter's retrospective exhibition, especially if the canvasses are displayed chronologically: one sees a certain style being adopted, and then explored, clarified and tested. It may be superficially tweaked (a different palette adopted, for example). But it's only rarely that one sees a radical transformation taking place. Similarly, the list of a scientist's research papers rarely includes a transformative contribution: mostly, scientists explore the implications of some already-accepted idea. Even if that idea is itself transformative, and relatively recent, it normally prompts exploration rather than further transformation. That was so in the case of ring-molecules, as we've seen; and the case history of the fullerenes provides further illustrations. Seldom does an individual scientist, or artist, make more than one transformative move. Picasso, who pioneered several distinct styles during his lifetime, is an example from the arts. In science, the Crick–Watson team discovered the double helix and, a few years later, the genetic code.

The saga of the fullerenes also illustrates the fact that identifying a 'creative' idea, or a scientific 'discovery', is not always straightforward. Such judgements can even be affected by national rivalries, not to mention social snobbery and personal jealousies (Schaffer 1994). The identification of creativity is never purely scientific. For, even though science can occasionally explain why we have certain values (shininess, for instance, see Boden 2006, 8.iv.c), it cannot, in principle, justify any value. Moreover, our values often change: different social groups/subgroups, in differing times and places, may value quite different things. Because the notion of *positive valuation* is included within the concept of creativity, the class of 'creative' ideas is not a natural kind. In other words, it is not a purely scientific concept.

It follows that neuroscience could never explain the origin of creative ideas without some prior (socially based) judgements identifying these ideas as creative, in contrast with others that are merely new. (Even novelty isn't always easily judged, as the case history of the fullerenes shows [Boden 2006, 1.iii.f–g]).

A final complication must be mentioned here: what we naturally think of as a 'single' idea or artefact may involve more than one sort of creativity. The three forms of creativity distinguished above are analytically distinct, in that they involve different types of psychological processes for generating novel ideas. But a given artwork or scientific theory can involve more than one type. That is partly why it is generally more sensible to ask whether this or that 'aspect' of the idea in question is creative, and in what way. A neuroscientific theory of creativity should be able to show how the three forms of creativity can be integrated, as well as how they can function independently.

III: What might neuroscience have to say?

There is no doubt that neuroscience could help to show how combinational creativity is possible. Indeed, it already has. Neurological studies, and computer models, of associative memory have already thrown light on the mechanisms underlying much poetic imagery.

The richness and subtlety of these associations have long been appreciated by literary scholars. The best example, here, is John Livingston Lowes's (1930) masterly literary detective story which traces the detailed origins of Samuel Taylor Coleridge's imagery in 'The Rime of the Ancient Mariner' and 'Kubla Khan' (Boden 2004, ch. 6). In relation to the pessimism about particularism expressed in Section

I, it is worth mentioning that Lowes had access not only to the whole of Coleridge's eclectic library but also to his commonplace books for the eighteen months during which these poems were written, in which Coleridge had jotted down quotations which had interested him. That degree of access to the detailed contents of another person's mind is highly unusual.

However, beyond the already long-familiar idea that brains are composed of interconnected units which are somehow responsible for conceptual associations (Hartley 1749), Lowes knew nothing of the neural mechanisms involved. Today, we are in a very different position. It was known by the 1980s that certain drugs can increase or decrease the associative range of conceptual thinking, leading to more or less inclusive and/or idiosyncratic combinations respectively (Shaw et al. 1986; cf. Eysenck 1994, 224–32). And now, we have much more data and many more neuroscientific (not least, neurocomputational) concepts, to work with.

This isn't to say that we can now come closer to literary particularism than Livingston Lowes, for instance, could. In other words, this does not mean that neuroscience could ever explain just how/why 'this' idea was associated with 'that' idea on a given occasion. Even if the idea in question could be neuronally located (as intentional verbs, for instance, have been located in the posterior superior temporal sulcus, or pSTS [Allison et al. 2000; Castelli et al. 2002; Frith and Frith 2003]), the specific association that arose in some individual's mind could not be explained in detail, still less, predicted. However, we saw in Section I that particularist explanation/prediction is not the aim of science. Insofar as such particularist insights are available, they are post hoc, not predictive, and are to be found rather in the humanities (John Livingston Lowes's discussion of 'The Rime of the Ancient Mariner' provides some exceptionally convincing examples).

Associative pathways, however, are not all there is to combinational creativity. There is also the tricky issue of 'relevance'. Conceivably, any concept could be associated with any other, by some sufficiently tortuous neuronal path. In that sense, there's no limit to the number of 'unfamiliar combinations' which are possible. But life is too short to follow only highly tortuous pathways. Even poets have to provide enough context to make their meaning communicable; and everyday speech, in general, has to be understood immediately. In other words, those novel combinations which we 'value', and therefore regard as 'creative', invariably involve relevance—even if the relevance is not immediately apparent.

An insightful computational approach to relevance suggests that we have evolved an involuntary, and exceptionless, principle of communication (and problem-solving) based on a cost–benefit analysis, weighing effort against effect (Sperber and Wilson 1986). The more information-processing effort it would take to bear *x* in mind in the context of *y*, the more costly it would be, and high cost gives low relevance. The more implications (regarding things of interest to the individual concerned) which would follow from considering *x*, the more effective it would be, and high effectiveness gives high relevance.

Paradoxically, the suggestion here is not that we pre-compute just how much effort/effect would be involved in considering a certain concept. Rather, there must be psychological mechanisms evolved for recognizing relevance. For example, our attention is naturally [*sic*] caught by movement, because moving things are often of interest. Similarly, even a newborn baby's attention is preferentially caught by human speech sounds. Besides being built into our sensory systems, relevance recognition is built into our memories: it's no accident, in this regard, that similar and/or frequently co-occurring memories are easily accessible, being 'stored' together in scripts, schemas and conceptual hierarchies.

Different cognitive strategies may vary in the measure of cost or benefit which they attach to a given conceptual 'distance'. Surrealists, for example, tolerate greater distances than straightforwardly 'representational' writers and painters do—hence the extreme unfamiliarity of the novel combinations found in their work. The artist's personal signature—which can affect many different aspects of a creative work (Boden 2010)—can apply here: one individual Surrealist may be more forgiving of conceptual distance than another. Similarly, different rhetorical styles in literature involve different levels of cost and/or different types of information processing in both writer and reader: compare Charles Dickens and James Joyce, for instance. A literary personal signature may also involve a preference for finding many sorts of relevance in certain concepts: animals, for the poet Ted Hughes, for example.

This analysis of relevance implies that, despite the claims of champions of symbolic computationalism such as Jerry Fodor (1983), laboured scientific inference is not a good model for daily, instantaneous, understanding (Sperber and Wilson 1986, 66–67). Similarly, it rejects the Good Old-Fashioned Artificial Intelligence (GOFAI) assumption that deliberate reasoning—which is needed by literary scholars and historians when puzzling over obscure texts—is required for spontaneous interpretation (75). Rather, our understanding typically depends on associative, non-logical, guessing that is constrained by what we take to be relevant.

It follows that a satisfactory neuroscientific account of combinational creativity would identify the various mechanisms evolved for judging relevance, given that this matter is a verbal/conceptual version of the notorious frame problem (Sperber and Wilson 1996; Boden 2006, 771–75, 1003–05), which is a tall order.

With respect to the other two forms of creativity, there's more bad news. For they are significantly less amenable to neuroscience. That's true in two ways.

First, we rarely know all the constraints defining the conceptual spaces of art or science, still less the computational processes required to explore and/or to transform them. Art historians and musicologists spend lifetimes attempting to make stylistic constraints explicit, and succeed only to a very limited degree. Sometimes, they even announce a given style to be unfathomable. For instance, an architectural historian specializing in Frank Lloyd Wright's work pronounced the style—the principle of 'balance'—of his Prairie Houses as being 'occult' (Hitchcock 1942).

One of the advantages of computer modelling is that it can sometimes help to develop, and to test, explicit theories about such matters. So, for instance, a computerized 'shape grammar' has generated every one of Wright's forty-or-so Prairie House designs, plus many others clearly sharing the same style, without ever producing one which lacks this intuitively recognizable principle of unity (Koning and Eizenberg 1981). Moreover, this work has shown that the 'fireplace' is the key to the style. That is, when generating specific design-choices, changes to the location of the fireplace (or to the number of fireplaces) result in changes to most other aspects of the house.

Second, even if we had defined the conceptual spaces concerned, and even if we knew the generative processes involved in negotiating and changing them, we wouldn't know how these are neurally embodied. We might assign them to some central cognitive workspace (Baars 1988; Changeux 2002), to be sure. And we might even be able to locate that workspace, very broadly, in the brain. But knowing just how the sonnet form, for instance, is neurally embodied, and how it is neurophysiologically accessed in generating 'Shall I compare thee to a Summer's day?' is way beyond the state of the art.

This is not just a difficulty in particularistic prediction, as discussed above: rather, the difficulty lies in knowing how it is possible for neurological mechanisms to implement the sonnet form, and to exploit it so as to generate the line in question. Similarly, explaining—in neurological terms—just how the Prairie House style can generate the

Henderson House, the Martin House or the Baker House (different examples, each named after the clients who commissioned them) is at present beyond us.

My own view is that it is likely to remain so for very many years, perhaps even forever. That's not because I agree with those philosophers (McGinn 1989, 1991) who argue that the explanation of high-level thought and consciousness is as far beyond the cognitive capacities of *Homo sapiens* as theoretical physics is beyond the capacities of squirrels and chimpanzees. I believe that position to be unnecessarily defeatist. Nevertheless, there are some fundamental problems here, which can't be solved by (theory-free) correlative brain-imaging, nor by reference, for example, to trial-and-error combinations and neural evolution (Changeux 1994).

One of these problems concerns the neural implementation of hierarchy. Most of the styles, or conceptual spaces, explored in art and science are hierarchical. The Prairie House fireplace, for instance, is the key to the genre because it lies at a fundamental level in the stylistic hierarchy (the 'space grammar') concerned, so that a decision about the fireplace will constrain many later decisions about other—superficially unrelated— matters. And the generating of 'Shall I compare thee to a Summer's day?' requires exploration of grammatical hierarchy. At present, we have no good ideas about how conceptual hierarchies are neurally embodied, nor how they can be rationally negotiated in creative thinking.

Still less do we know how transformational procedures may be embodied which can alter those hierarchies. Even domain-general transformations (such as, 'consider the negative' or 'drop a constraint') are a mystery. And the neural basis of the many domain-specific procedures which led from early Renaissance music (broadly, one composition, one key), through increasingly daring modulations and harmonies, to atonal music is even more elusive (Rosen 1976; Boden 2004, 71–74).

One might suggest, at this point, that computer simulation could help. And, in principle, it could. However, a neuroscientifically plausible model is going to be connectionist rather than symbolic. Yet, only symbolic models (aka GOFAI) (Haugeland 1985, 112) are well suited to represent hierarchy. Connectionist models, in general, are not.

Despite heroic efforts in that direction, this problem has not yet been solved (Boden 2006, 12.viii). Perhaps the most impressive attempt is the harmony theory (Smolensky et al. 1993; Smolensky and Legendre 2006), which draws on neuroscientific knowledge. However, this was specifically developed to deal with grammatical hierarchy (syntax), and it is not clear how it can be generalized to model conceptual hierarchies such as, artistic/scientific styles.

Even if it could, there would be a huge gap between harmony-theoretic modelling and neurological reality. Most connectionist models, especially those intended as models of psychological (not just neurological) functions, rely on computational units which, as compared with real neurons, are too neat, too simple, too few and too 'dry' (Boden 2006, 14.ii). In brief, the networks studied by connectionist AI are very non-neural nets.

To be sure, connectionism is becoming gradually more realistic. One recent textbook, featuring the Leabra software system developed by its authors, makes great efforts to integrate connectionist AI with neuroscience (O'Reilly and Munakata 2000). For example, the activation function which controls the spiking of the simulated neurons in Leabra is only 'occasionally' drawn from mathematical connectionism (42). Usually, it is based on facts about the biological machinery for producing a spike, including detailed data on ion channels, membrane potentials, conductance, leakages and other electrical properties of nerve cells (32–48). Similarly, the basic equations used by Leabra when simulating high-level phenomena, such as reading or conceptual memory, are (usually) painstakingly drawn from detailed biophysical data. This is true, for example, of the equation used for integrating many inputs into a single neuron (see the authors' explanation of equation 2.8 on pp. 37ff.).

The Leabra authors drew the line at applying this equation 'at every point along the dendrites and cell body of the neuron, along with additional equations that specify how the membrane potential spreads along neighbouring points of the neuron' (38). They had no wish 'to implement hundreds or thousands of equations to implement a single neuron', so they used an approximating equation instead. But, characteristically, they provided references to other books which did explain how to implement such detailed single-neuron simulations.

In general, the psychological models developed by O'Reilly and Munakata would have been different had the neuroscientific data been different. Their discussion of dyslexia, for instance, built not only on previous connectionist work (Plaut and Shallice 1993; Plaut et al. 1996), but also on recent clinical and neurological information (331–41). As our knowledge of the brain advances, future psychological models, so they believe, will, or anyway should, be different again. They see their book as 'a "first draft" of a coherent framework for computational cognitive neuroscience' (11).

As regards creativity, this implies that we may hope for future connectionist models which embody specific neuroscientific data as well as a better understanding of the complex computational processes involved in all three types of creativity. But to hope is not to have. (And I'm not holding my breath.)

IV: Wittgenstein and neuroscience

I've assumed so far that it is coherent to aim for a neuroscientific explanation of creativity and, for that matter, of any other psychological phenomenon. In other words, such an explanation is possible in principle, irrespective of whether it has been—or is ever likely to be—achieved. And I've written as though the only reason for denying this is the mysterian view that there is something essentially quasi-magical about creativity, which puts it beyond the reach of science. However, many philosophers of mind would deny the possibility of a scientific understanding of creativity—and of any other psychological phenomenon—on very different grounds. These writers include the followers of Ludwig Wittgenstein, who suggested in his *Philosophical Investigations* (1953) that there is no level of psychological explanation between remarks about conscious phenomenology and observations about the physical mechanisms of the brain. So, for instance, Richard Rorty explicitly looked forward to 'the disappearance of psychology as a discipline distinct from neurology' (1979, 121).

Wittgensteinians in general reject psychological explanations posed at the sub-personal level, and therefore criticize those neuroscientific theories which define brain-processes cognitively (or computationally), rather than purely neurologically. They accuse neuroscientists of incoherence due to the 'mereological fallacy', which is to attribute to a part of a system some predicate which is properly attributed only to the whole (Bennett and Hacker 2003). In this context, the 'system' in question is the whole person, the 'parts' are the brain (or parts thereof), and the 'predicates' are psychological terms, such as knowledge, memory, belief, reasoning, choice and, of course, creativity.

With this view, there is absolutely no hope of a naturalistic psychology. Insofar as psychology exists as a scientific discipline, it is said to be a hermeneutic, not a natural science (cf. McDowell 1994; Harre 2002). So, neuroscience could never 'replace' psychology, in the sense of substituting for it. At most, a (non-cognitivist) neuroscience could compensate for the lack of a cognitivist (sub-personal) psychology.

This rejection of naturalism in psychology reflects a deep divide in Western philosophy, into which we can't go here (but see Boden 2006, 16.vi–viii). A few neuroscientists (such as followers of Humberto Maturana and Francisco

Varela 1980) lie on the anti-naturalist side of the divide. But the vast majority does not. Moreover, neuroscience itself has become increasingly cognitivist—indeed, computational—since the 1950s (Boden 2006, ch. 14). Information-processes and computational mechanisms are now considered crucial in many neuroscientific explanations, from studies of vision to the higher thought processes. And this paper has argued that the computational level of theorizing is crucial in explaining creativity, too.

So, although Wittgenstein might seem at first sight to be the neuroscientist's friend, perhaps he is not such a good friend after all. Not a false friend, to be sure—for that would involve insincerity or betrayal. But, in my view, a mistaken one.

V: Conclusion

Nothing that has been said above suggests that there can never be a neuroscience of creativity. Indeed, a neuroscience of combinational creativity is arguably within sight, if not within reach.

It is not yet within reach, partly because—as explained in Section III—there are challenging problems concerning how we make judgements of 'relevance' when engaging in, or appreciating, combinational creativity. A neuroscientific explanation of that is not within sight. Moreover, given that this is a verbal/conceptual version of the notorious frame problem (Sperber and Wilson 1996; Boden 2006, 771–75, 1003–05), it is a tall order.

Further reasons why a neuroscience of creativity is not within reach involve hierarchy, as we have seen. Clearly, it must be possible, somehow, for hierarchy—and all other aspects of symbolic thinking—to be implemented in (broadly) connectionist systems. After all, the human brain is such a system. However, we need to understand, much better than we do at present, how a basically connectionist system can emulate a symbolic one; that is, how connectionism can emulate a von Neumann machine.

In addition to highly general questions such as that one, we need to focus on the specific structure of—and the generative processes within—the myriad conceptual spaces underlying science and art. For, neither exploratory nor transformational creativity can be properly understood without taking those computational features into account.

References

Allison, T., A. Puce and G. McCarthy. 2000. 'Social Perception from Visual Cues: Role of the STS Region.' *Trends in Cognitive Sciences* 4 (7): 267–78.

Baars, B.J. 1988. *A Cognitive Theory of Consciousness*. Cambridge: Cambridge University Press.

Bennett, M.R., and P.M.S. Hacker. 2003. *Philosophical Foundations of Neuroscience*. Oxford: Blackwell.

Boden, M.A. 2004. *The Creative Mind: Myths and Mechanisms*. Second ed., expanded/revised, London: Routledge. First ed., London: Weidenfeld & Nicolson, 1990.

———. 2006. *Mind as Machine: A History of Cognitive Science*. Oxford: Clarendon Press.

———. 2010. 'Personal Signatures in Art.' In *Creativity and Art: Three Roads to Surprise*, 92–124. Oxford: Oxford University Press.

Castelli, F., C.D. Frith, F. Happe and U. Frith. 2002. 'Autism, Asperger Syndrome, and Brain Mechanisms for the Attribution of Mental States to Animated Shapes.' *Brain* 125: 1839–49.

Changeux, J.-P. 1994. 'Creative Processes: Art and Neuroscience.' *Leonardo* 27 (3): 189–201.

———. 2002. *The Physiology of Truth: Neuroscience and Human Knowledge*. Translated by M.B. DeBevoise. Cambridge, MA: Harvard University Press.

Eysenck, H.J. 1994. 'The Measurement of Creativity.' In *Dimensions of Creativity*, edited by M.A. Boden, 199–242. Cambridge, MA: MIT Press.

Fodor, J.A. 1983. *The Modularity of Mind: An Essay in Faculty Psychology*. Cambridge, MA: MIT Press.

Frith, U., and C.D. Frith. 2003. 'Development and Neurophysiology of Mentalizing.' *Philosophical Transactions of the Royal Society of London B* 358: 459–73.

Harre, R.M. 2002. *Cognitive Science: A Philosophical Introduction.* London: Sage.

Hartley, D. 1749. *Observations on Man: His Frame, His Duty, and His Expectations.* London. (Facsimile reproduction edited by T.L. Huguelet, reprinted Gainesville, Florida: Scholars' Facsimiles and Reprints, 1966.)

Haugeland, J. 1985. *Artificial Intelligence: The Very Idea.* Cambridge, MA: MIT Press.

Hitchcock, H.R. 1942. *In the Nature of Materials: The Buildings of Frank Lloyd Wright; 1887–1941.* New York: Meredith Press.

Jones, D.E.H. 'Daedalus'. 1966. 'Note in Ariadne column.' *New Scientist,* 32. 3 November: 245.

————. 1982. *The Inventions of Daedalus.* Oxford: W.H. Freeman.

Koch, C., and I. Segev. eds. 1989. *Methods in Neuronal Modeling: From Synapses to Networks.* Cambridge, MA: MIT Press.

Koning, H., and J. Eizenberg. 1981. 'The Language of the Prairie: Frank Lloyd Wright's Prairie Houses.' *Environment and Planning B* 8: 295–323.

Kroto, H.W., J.R. Heath, S.C. O'Brien, R.F. Curl and R.E. Smalley. 1985. 'C60: Buckminsterfullerene.' *Nature* 318 (6042): 162–63.

Lowes, J.L. 1930. *The Road to Xanadu: A Study in the Ways of the Imagination.* London: Houghton. Revised ed., 1951.

Maturana, H.R., and F.J. Varela. 1980. *Autopoiesis and Cognition: The Realization of the Living.* Boston: Reidel. First published in Spanish, 1972.

Mayhew, J.E.W. 1983. 'Stereopsis.' In *Physical and Biological Processing of Images*, edited by O.J. Bradick and A.C. Sleigh, 204–16. New York: Springer-Verlag.

McDowell, J. 1994. *Mind and World*. Cambridge, MA: Harvard University Press.

McGinn, C. 1989. 'Can We Solve the Mind–Body Problem?' *Mind* 98: 349–66.

————. 1991. *The Problem of Consciousness*. Oxford: Basil Blackwell.

Meehl, P.E. 1954. *Clinical Versus Statistical Prediction: A Theoretical Analysis and a Review of the Evidence*. Minneapolis: University of Minnesota Press.

O'Reilly, R.C., and Y. Munakata. 2000. *Computational Explorations in Cognitive Neuroscience: Understanding the Mind by Simulating the Brain*. Cambridge, MA: MIT Press.

Plaut, D.C., J.L. McClelland, M.S. Seidenberg and K. Patterson. 1996. 'Understanding Normal and Impaired Word Reading: Computational Principles in Quasi-Regular Domains.' *Psychological Review* 103: 56–115.

Plaut, D.C., and T. Shallice. 1993. 'Deep Dyslexia: A Case Study of Connectionist Neuropsychology.' *Cognitive Neuropsychology* 10: 377–500.

Rorty, R. 1979. *Philosophy and the Mirror of Nature*. Princeton, NJ: Princeton University Press.

Rosen, C. 1976. *Schoenberg*. Glasgow: Collins.

Schaffer, S. 1994. 'Making Up Discovery.' In *Dimensions of Creativity*, edited by M.A. Boden, 14–51. Cambridge, MA: MIT Press.

Shaw, E.D., J.J. Mann and P.E. Stokes. 1986. 'Effects of Lithium Carbonate on Creativity in Nobel Bipolar Outpatients.' *American Journal of Psychiatry* 143: 1166–69.

Smalley, R.E. 1996. 'Discovering the Fullerenes.' *Reviews of Modern Physics* 69 (3): 723–30. (Nobel Prize acceptance speech.)

Smolensky, P., and G. Legendre. 2006. *The Harmonic Mind: From Neural Computation to Optimality-Theoretic Grammar.* 2 vols. Cambridge, MA: MIT Press.

Smolensky, P., G. Legendre and Y. Miyata. 1993. 'Integrating Connectionist and Symbolic Computation for the Theory of Language.' *Current Science* 64: 381–91.

Sperber, D., and D. Wilson. 1986. *Relevance: Communication and Cognition.* Oxford: Blackwell.

———. 1996. 'Fodor's Frame Problem and Relevance Theory.' *Behavioral and Brain Sciences* 19: 530–32.

Wittgenstein, L. 1953. *Philosophical Investigations.* Translated by G.E.M. Anscombe. Oxford: Blackwell.

From Creative Writer to Creativity Researcher: Exploring Ways to Study the Field

James C. Kaufman

For the first two decades of my life, I wanted to be a creative writer. I tried to write anything and everything—poems, stories, plays, newspaper articles, non-fiction and about sports. I did a double major in college—creative writing and, as an afterthought, psychology. I ended up pursuing psychology, in part because I realized I could have more luck and be better able to support myself as a creative psychologist than as a creative writer.

Yet my strong interest in creative writing permeated much of my subsequent career. My first master's thesis—later, one of my first published papers (Kaufman 2002a)—was an overview of past research on writers. My dissertation

(Kaufman 2002b) examined the differences in thinking styles and personality between creative writers and journalists. And one of my first large research projects was a historiometric investigation of eminent writers and mental illness (Kaufman 2001).

Even beyond this initial burst, however, the insights and ideas from my pursuit of creative writing have continued to play into my career as a researcher. For example, when I wrote actively, I would write nearly anything. I wrote articles for the local newspaper about high school sports. I wrote humorous parodies for local underground zines. My father and I did research on baseball and wrote articles about our findings. I wrote short horror stories, poetry, serious prose and, eventually, plays and musicals. Nonetheless, I tended to stick to the larger domain of writing. I showed virtually no aptitude for music or art. Could I have been successful if I had tried a radically different domain as a creative outlet?

This question taps into a hot topic about whether there is a general creativity factor. If creativity is such a thing, then, Mark Zuckerberg would have become a creative superstar in whichever area he ended up pursuing. If Zuckerberg hadn't created Facebook, he might have written a classic opera or discovered a new element. If there is no general creativity factor—if creativity is domain-specific—then, the abilities and predispositions that led to Zuckerberg's being a success in the social media world would not necessarily have translated to other fields.

With John Baer, I have developed the Amusement Park Theoretical (APT) model of creativity to integrate generalist and domain-specific views of creativity. We are not the first to try to synthesize these ideas. Others, for example, have proposed a 'hybrid' view in which creativity is primarily general but appears domain-specific in 'real world' performance (Plucker and Beghetto 2004). According to this theory, the level of specificity changes with the social context, and matures as a person advances from childhood into adulthood.

The details of the model are presented elsewhere (Baer and Kaufman 2005a, 2005b; Kaufman and Baer 2004, 2005, 2006), so I will summarize the main tenets. The APT model is based on the metaphor of a large amusement park. In an amusement park, there are 'initial requirements' which apply to all areas of the park. You need a way to travel to the park, you need a ticket to be admitted, and so on. Similarly, there are initial requirements which, to varying degrees, are necessary to be creative in any domain. For example, in order to be creative at something, you must have a certain basic amount of intelligence. You need to be driven to do something creative, regardless of which factors motivate you. Finally, you should be in an environment which enables—and, ideally, nurtures—creative expression. These three are the initial requirements for any attempt at creativity to succeed. They are by no means the only initial requirements, but they are the three key ones that the APT model highlights.

As we have discussed in other papers (Kaufman and Baer 2004; Baer and Kaufman 2005a, 2005b), amusement parks also have 'general thematic areas'. At Disney World, one might select from among Epcot, the Magic Kingdom, the Animal Kingdom and the Hollywood Studios. Similarly, there are several different broad areas in which someone could be creative. Such areas might be comparable to Gardner's (1999) eight intelligences: bodily-kinesthetic, interpersonal, intrapersonal, language, logical-mathematical, musical, naturalistic and spatial. Or, Holland's (1997) model of vocational interests: realistic, investigative, artistic, social, enterprising and conventional. Kaufman (2012), in examining self-assessments across multiple creative domains, found five general thematic areas: art, performance, science, scholarship and everyday life.

Once you arrive at a particular park, there are sections within: Discovery Island, DinoLand and Rifiki's Planet Watch are all found in the Animal Kingdom. Similarly, there are 'domains' of creativity within larger general thematic areas—e.g., biology and chemistry are domains within the general thematic area of science. These domains in turn can be subdivided into 'microdomains'—e.g., the Conservation Station and the Wildlife Express Train are both part of Rifiki's Plant Watch. In the domain of psychology, one might specialize in the microdomain of clinical psychology or organizational psychology. Although the initial requirements are spelled out only for the beginning of the model, there are clearly requirements for every descending level. Lubinski and Benbow (2006) argue that personal attributes—abilities and interests—and the environment are of equal importance in determining success and satisfaction. The more one's abilities and interests match the requirements of the environment, the better.

For example, if one were interested in assessing the creative abilities of a subject in terms of creativity in writing poetry, one might start by assessing such initial requirements as a certain minimal level of intelligence and appropriate motivation and environment, as well as skill in the general thematic area of writing. Next, one might assess skills in certain domains specially relevant to poetry, such as vocabulary, metaphor-making or skill with language. Finally, if one were interested only in the ability to write haiku, for example, then, one would look for the specific microdomain.

If, on the other hand, one were interested in a student's creative potential in the area of advertising, the hierarchy of skills that one would evaluate would be quite different. The initial requirements, such as motivation, might be similar but skills from a different general thematic area would be of interest; for example, social/interpersonal skills would be more important. The differences would become even greater as one moved down the hierarchy to domains and microdomains.

Motivation could also be assessed at different levels of such a hierarchy. For example, a student might have strong intrinsic motivation at the level of the general thematic area of art, and this would indicate a tendency toward creative productivity in the arts in general. On the other hand, another student may have extremely high intrinsic motivation only in the domain of sculpture, which predicts a greater likelihood of creativity in that domain but not in other arts. Or a student's interest at a given point in time might be even more narrowly focused on a microdomain—a student may have great interest in making sculptures out of a particular type of wood but be uninterested in other media.

People who pursue different general thematic areas may have different personalities. For example, Furnham, Batey, Booth, Patel and Lozinskaya (2011) examined creativity in arts and science students, and found that arts students had more self-reported creative accomplishments and higher self-assessed creativity, although there were no differences on a divergent thinking measure. They then examined students majoring in arts, natural sciences and social sciences. They found similar results—arts students rated themselves as more creative, but there were no differences in measured creativity.

How easy is it to move from one domain to another? As I have mentioned, in my days as a young creative writer, I was able to move fairly quickly from short stories to poetry to brief humour pieces to plays. Yet, as a psychologist, it is a different story. I have a hard-enough time shifting from a journal article to a blog. In addition, my primary subject matter is creativity. I may expand a little: sometimes I write about related constructs, such as motivation or personality, but most of my papers are about the same topic. Why?

One answer can be found in my level of experience and accomplishment: I never developed much beyond the level of amateur writer. My poems and stories were published in small magazines and my plays were produced in small theatres, but I never became a professional. A different model—which I developed with Ron Beghetto—may explain why I was able to reach out across domains at a lower level yet find it much more difficult now that I am a professional.

Our Four C Model of creativity (Beghetto and Kaufman 2007, 2009, 2013; Kaufman and Beghetto 2009; Kaufman, Beghetto, Baer and Ivcevic 2010) grew out of a desire to expand the predominant dichotomous view of creativity in the field. The two primary approaches to creativity were Big-C creativity and little-c creativity (Csikszentmihalyi 1996). Big-C focuses on eminent creativity. The goals of this approach are often to learn about creative genius and to discuss which creative works may last forever, e.g., Simonton (2009). Big-C creators are extremely prodigious in their achievements, have been recognized as revolutionary by gatekeepers of a domain (Csikszentmihalyi 1996), and have made landmark contributions. Creative greatness may be studied by analysing the lives of well-known creators, or interviewing renowned individuals, or by studying people who excel at high levels on creativity measures. Big-C creativity has, traditionally, been the focus of much research and theorizing in creativity studies.

Another perspective is to focus on little-c, or everyday creativity. Little-c is creativity inherent in the daily activities and experiences in which the average person may participate. Areas of research which focus on little-c creativity may be aimed at developing and warranting the assertion that creative potential is widely distributed (Richards 2007). If Big-C creativity might compose a brilliant symphony, little-c might sing a song at a talent show. Ron Beghetto and I added two categories: mini-c and Pro-c.

Mini-c creativity consists of self-discoveries—the novel and personally meaningful insights and interpretations inherent in the learning process. Someone may experience mini-c any time he tries something new. Merely cooking a new meal may result in many mini-c thoughts. At the mini-c level, creativity is not necessarily a product, nor may it seem even to be something new or useful to another person. It may be new and useful only to the person with the idea.

Indeed, the definition of mini-c creativity (Beghetto and Kaufman 2007) stresses the importance of the personal judgement of novelty and meaningfulness. This focus on subjective judgement distinguishes mini-c creativity from more objective expressions of creativity in which the novelty and meaningfulness of the outcome requires external judgement. Consequently, mini-c insights may never go beyond the individual creator. Yet, although mini-c creativity may not meet with the traditional standards used for judging Big-C or even little-c creativity—that is, the production of a product which is externally judged as being novel and meaningful (see Kaufman 2009)—mini-c creativity can and should be considered a sign of creative potential.

Pro-c represents professional-level creators who have not yet achieved the genius or legendary status of Big-C. People at the Pro-c level are experienced professionals who can create at a high level and can likely support themselves through this activity. One of the biggest distinctions between Pro-c and Big-C is the perspective of time. From the appropriate distance and context, some composers— such as Mozart or Beethoven—stand out as being among the best in the world. Other composers may be highly accomplished and may have been well regarded in their day, but are clearly not in the pantheon of all-time greats.

To put everything in perspective, a child who learns a new way of painting a picture—perhaps by using the tip of a paintbrush—may experience mini-c. As he continues painting, he may show his artwork to his parents, his teachers and his friends. He may grow to a point where other people like his painting and recognize it as creative; at this point, he can be said to be little-c. If he decides to pursue art as a career—or as an immersive hobby— he will develop experience with each additional hour dedicated to his craft. He will likely reach some level of success: whether he sells many paintings or very few, he has acquired a certain amount of professional expertise and may be considered to be Pro-c. If his work is exceptionally creative—to the point of being remembered and discussed and analysed many years hence—then, he may reach the Big-C pinnacle.

When I was a creative writer, I was shifting from the mini-c to the little-c level. I was trying out new styles and techniques and genres. I was still learning. As a result, it was easier for me to shift gears. Why? As creativity increases on the spectrum of accomplishment and experience, domain-specificity increases. One reason for this is that creativity requires a vast amount of background knowledge within a domain. This process of acquiring expertise in an area requires approximately ten years from entering a field to making any kind of substantial contribution (Ericsson, Roring and Nandagopal 2007; Hayes 1989). These ten years are spent learning the mechanics of the field, discovering all the practical issues which cannot be taught in a book, and obsessively plying one's trade. These ten years do not represent a basic apprenticeship, as in being taught how to mend clothes. Rather, these are years of active experimentation and generation of new ideas (Gardner 1993). If I had pursued creative writing and received my MFA (master of fine arts), I would have been working my way up towards Pro-c, and I may have found it harder to shift between different genres.

Now that I am a psychologist, I have, hopefully, reached Pro-c. At this level—and even more so at the Big-C level—it is much harder to be creative in multiple domains. Indeed, it is surprising how hard it is to think of true 'Renaissance' people. Some names of people who have reached Big-C across multiple domains may come to mind: Leonardo da Vinci; Benjamin Franklin; Paul Robeson; Bertrand Russell; Marie Curie (Physics and Chemistry) and Linus Pauling (Chemistry and Peace), who won Nobel Prizes in two different categories. But truly, there are not very many of them.

However, there are many advantages in growing more experienced. One thing I would like to think is that I have got better at determining the creativity of my work. When I used to write stories and plays, I would often finish something that I thought was wonderful, only to have my peers, teachers or editors think quite differently. Now, I have grown better at figuring out how good—or creative—my work is. I am rarely shocked by the outcome of a paper submission or by how the field reacts to a new theory or finding.

This ability is related to what Ron Beghetto and I have called creative metacognition (CMC) (Kaufman and Beghetto

2013; see also Beghetto and Kaufman 2014). Like other forms of metacognitive knowledge, creative metacognition is a special form of cognition which helps people monitor and develop their creative competence. Consistent with the conceptions of metacognitive knowledge of previous scholars (Flavell 1979; Pintrich, Wolters and Baxter 2000), we have defined creative metacognition as a combination of creative self-knowledge—knowing one's own creative strengths and limitations, both within a domain and as a general trait—and contextual knowledge—knowing when, where, how and why to be creative.

The topic of creative metacognition, which is one of the core research questions I have been asking recently, is again particularly close to my heart because of my creative writing background. When I was a junior in college, I decided to apply for graduate school. I sent away for application packages from both psychology PhD programmes and creative writing MFA programmes. One of the MFA packages said, in essence, that if you could do anything else other than write, then, you should do that thing. They graduate a specific number of creative writing MFAs each year, and the jobs available were just barely enough for their graduates (leaving aside all the other MFAs). I had enough creative metacognition to realize that although I had had some early success as a writer, I could succeed elsewhere. I applied my passion in creativity to the psychological realm, where I like to think I have had a larger impact than if I had been still working on my stories and plays.

References

Baer, J., and J.C. Kaufman. 2005a. 'Bridging Generality and Specificity: The Amusement Park Theoretical (APT) Model of Creativity.' *Roeper Review* 27: 158–63.

———. 2005b. 'Whence Creativity? Overlapping and Dual-aspect Skills and Traits.' In *Creativity Across Domains: Faces of the Muse*, edited by J.C. Kaufman and J. Baer Mahwah, 313–20. NJ: Lawrence Erlbaum.

Beghetto, R.A., and J.C. Kaufman. 2007. 'Toward a Broader Conception of Creativity: A Case for "mini-c" Creativity.' *Psychology of Aesthetics, Creativity, and the Arts* 1: 13–79.

———. 2009. 'Intellectual Estuaries: Connecting Learning and Creativity in Programs of Advanced Academics.' *Journal of Advanced Academics* 20: 296–324.

———. 2013. 'Creativity: Five Fundamental Insights that Every Educator Should Know.' *Educational Leadership* 70: 10–15.

———. 2014. 'Classroom contexts for creativity.' *High Ability Studies* 25: 53-69.

Csikszentmihalyi, M. 1996. *Creativity: Flow and the Psychology of Discovery and Invention*. New York: HarperCollins.

Ericsson, K., R.W. Roring and K. Nandagopal. 2007. 'Giftedness and Evidence for Reproducibly Superior performance: An

Account Based on the Expert Performance Framework.' *High Ability Studies* 18: 3–56

Flavell, J. 1979. 'Metacognition and Cognitive Monitoring: A New Area of Cognitive-Developmental Inquiry.' *American Psychologist* 34: 906–11.

Furnham, A., M. Batey, T.W. Booth, V.Patel and D. Lozinskaya. 2011. 'Individual Difference Predictors of Creativity in Art and Science Students.' *Thinking Skills and Creativity* 6: 114–21.

Gardner, H. 1993. *Creating Minds*. New York: Basic Books.

———. 1999. *Intelligence Reframed: Multiple Intelligences for the 21st Century*. New York: Basic Books.

Hayes, J.R. 1989. 'Cognitive Processes in Creativity.' In *Handbook of Creativity*, edited by J.A. Glover, R.R. Ronning and C.R. Reynolds, 135–45. New York: Plenum Press.

Holland, J.L. 1997. *Making Vocational Choices: A Theory of Vocational Personalities and Work Environments* (3rd ed.). Odessa, FL: Psychological Assessment Resources.

Kaufman, J.C. 2001. 'The Sylvia Plath Effect: Mental Illness in Eminent Creative Writers.' *Journal of Creative Behavior* 35: 37–50.

———. 2002a. 'Dissecting the Golden Goose: Components of Studying Creative Writers.' *Creativity Research Journal* 14: 27–40.

———. 2002b. 'Narrative and Paradigmatic Thinking Styles in Creative Writing and Journalism Students.' *Journal of Creative Behavior* 36: 201–20.

————. 2009. Creativity 101. New York: Springer.

————. 2012. 'Counting the Muses: Development of the Kaufman-Domains of Creativity Scale (K-DOCS).' *Psychology of Aesthetics, Creativity, and the Arts* 6: 298–308.

Kaufman, J.C., and J. Baer. 2004. 'Hawking's Haiku, Madonna's Math.' In *Creativity: From Potential to Realization*, edited by R.J. Sternberg, E.L. Grigorenko and J.L. Singer, 3–20. Washington, DC: American Psychological Association.

————. 2005. 'The Amusement Park Theory of Creativity.' In *Creativity Across Domains: Faces of the Muse*, edited by J.C. Kaufman and J. Baer, 321–28. Mahwah, NJ: Lawrence Erlbaum.

————. 2006. 'Intelligent Testing with Torrance.' *Creativity Research Journal* 18: 99–102.

Kaufman, J.C., and R.A. Beghetto. 2009. 'Beyond Big and Little: The Four C Model of Creativity.' *Review of General Psychology* 13: 1–12.

Kaufman, J. C., and R.A. Beghetto. 2013. 'In Praise of Clark Kent: Creative Metacognition and the Importance of Teaching Kids When (Not) to Be Creative.' *Roeper Review* 35: 155-165.

Kaufman, J.C., R.A. Beghetto, J. Baer and Z. Ivcevic. 2010. 'Creativity Polymathy: What Benjamin Franklin Can Teach Your Kindergartener.' *Learning and Individual Differences* 20: 380–87.

Lubinski, D., and C.P. Benbow. 2006. 'Study of Mathematically Precocious Youth after 35 Years: Uncovering Antecedents for the Development of Math-Science Expertise.' *Perspectives on Psychological Science* 1: 316-345.

Pintrich, P.R., C. Wolters and G. Baxter. 2000. 'Assessing Metacognition and Self-regulated Learning.' In *Issues in the Measurement of Metacognition*, edited by G. Schraw and J. Impara, 43–97. Lincoln, NE: Buros Institute of Mental Measurements.

Plucker, J.A., and R.A. Beghetto. 2004. 'Why Creativity is Domain-General, Why It Looks Domain-Specific, and Why the Distinction Doesn't Matter.' In *Creativity: From Potential to Realization*, edited by R.J. Sternberg, E.L. Grigorenko and J.L. Singer, 153–68. Washington, DC: American Psychological Association Press.

Richards, R, ed. 2007. *Everyday Creativity and New Views of Human Nature: Psychological, Social, and Spiritual Perspectives*. Washington, DC: American Psychological Association Press.

Simonton, D.K. 2009. *Genius 101*. New York: Springer.

More from the 'Boundaries of Consciousness' series

On Dreams and Dreaming

Edited by Sudhir Kakar

Mapping the uncharted territory at the edges of psychological knowledge, these fascinating essays explore compelling aspects of dreams and dreaming. They discuss topics as diverse as memorable dreams, lucid dreaming, the role of dreams in the evolution of human consciousness and the relationship between dreams and the waking state.

In 'The Dream and Its Embedding', psychoanalyst Patrick Mahony demonstrates, with absorbing case studies, how dreams can become effective therapeutic tools while dream scholar Kelly Bulkely concludes in 'Big Dreams' that, ultimately, the function of dreams is to make the brain grow. Luigi Zoja, dream analyst, explores the profusion of nightmares among soldiers, prisoners and other victims of war in 'Nightmares'. And Madhu Tandan, who lived for seven years in an ashram at the foothills of the Himalayas, explains how dreams can access a level of consciousness beyond the psychological.

This volume is the first in the 'Boundaries of Consciousness' series, which, under the leadership of Sudhir Kakar, seeks to bring together psychoanalysts, philosophers, religious-studies scholars and neuroscientists in order to expand the frontiers of current psychological understanding.

On Dreams and Dreaming will be of interest to scholars and to all who dream and seek to understand why.

More from the 'Boundaries of Consciousness' series

Seriously Strange: Thinking Anew about Psychical Experiences

Edited by Sudhir Kakar and Jeffrey J. Kripal

Despite being sullied by frauds and dismissed by sceptics, the paranormal has exerted a strange fascination over humankind for centuries. In *Seriously Strange*, a group of nine intellectuals come together to shed light on some of the most baffling experiences on record—psychical experiences.

Through these illuminating essays, they tell us how such extraordinary events can be decoded and interpreted to become the object of rigorous scientific study. The range is wide: from essays that reveal how Freud and Jung engaged with the notion of the paranormal to a provocative and humorous memoir of a physicist who spent over a decade running a secret psychic spying programme for the US government during the Cold War; from heartfelt accounts by practising psychiatrists of the anomalies in their healing practice to a learned call for the renewal of professional parapsychology in the light of Patanjali's *Yoga Sutras*.

By telling their own stories and exploring some of the implications of their work, these men and women map the mind-bending geography of the human psyche and the spectrum of experiences—love and death, desire and sex, hurt and healing, myth and magic—that influence it.

More from the 'Boundaries of Consciousness' series

Death and Dying

Edited by Sudhir Kakar

Billions have died in the thousands of years since human beings first developed language but we do not have a single credible account of the subjective experience of dying and the afterlife. This is why death continues to be an immense mystery and a subject of eternal fascination.

In *Death and Dying*, scholars and intellectuals illumine the major issues raised by the inevitable ending to life. The range is wide: from the dread that accompanies all notions of mortality to the objective evidence for the existence of an afterlife; from an exploration of the spiritual dimensions of mourning to analyses of how death was perceived and interpreted by geniuses like John Keats, Rabindranath Tagore and Carl Jung.

Utterly compelling, these essays prompt us to question our fears and notions of death while enabling us to perceive this phenomenon with greater understanding and intelligence.